WHISPERS OF WISDOM WITH A TWIST

GRANDMA'S TIMELESS ADVICE FOR LIFE'S JOURNEY

DANIA ALEN

MIRACLES FROM D'HEART

Whispers of Wisdom
With a Twist
Grandma's Timeless Advice for Life's Journey

Published by
Miracles from D'Heart
Miami, Florida

ISBNs

Print: 979-8-9940064-0-5
Ebook: 979-8-9940064-1-2

Subjects:
'5000 HUMOR / Form / Anecdotes, Epigrams & Quotations
'L031000   SELF-HELP / Personal Growth / General
)21000   SELF-HELP / Motivational & Inspirational

Printed in the United States

'lum

INTRODUCTION

Welcome to *Whispers of Wisdom With a Twist: Grandma's Timeless Advice for Life's Journey*, where love is baked into every memory, wisdom comes with a wink, and life lessons are served with a side of laughter.

This book isn't a tale; it's a toolkit for navigating life. A guide drawn from years of living, learning, and laughing through the chaos. Inside these pages, you won't find dramatic plot twists or sweeping narratives. You'll find something better: real, practical wisdom gathered one moment, one mistake, and one breakthrough at a time.

This book is my way of passing down the kind of advice that doesn't shout but simply nudges. It's the quiet kind that shows up when you need it most, like a well-timed reminder or a loving nudge from someone who's been there. Whether you're facing a fork in the road or just trying to make it through Monday, there's something here for you.

I wrote this with my children in mind, but it's for anyone who's ever wished life came with a cheat sheet. Think of it as a collection of "I wish someone had told me" moments, served with warmth, wit, and just enough sass to keep things interesting.

You'll find reflections, gentle truths, and a few laugh-out-loud lessons that prove wisdom doesn't always wear a serious face. And don't miss the bonus section at the end, where my court reporting adventures and a couple of other stories add a splash of humor to the mix.

So, pull up a chair. Let's talk life, love, and the little things that make all the difference.

A Thoughtful Disclaimer

Before we begin, a gentle heads-up: If heartfelt reflections, light humor, or the occasional "back in my day" story aren't your cup of tea, consider this your friendly warning. But if you're open to a little soul-soothing wisdom served with a wink and a warm heart, you're in the right place.

This book is not intended to diagnose, treat, or heal. The insights shared here are simply personal reflections, advice from my heart, not prescriptions for yours. If you're navigating something that requires deeper support, I wholeheartedly encourage you to seek guidance from a qualified professional.

DEDICATION

This book is lovingly dedicated to my parents. (*Gracias, mami y papi, por ser exactamente lo que he necesitado en esta vida. Los quiero mucho*). To my brother, his wife, my three nieces (plus their husbands and six energetic little humans), my aunts and uncles, and roughly forty first cousins—some of whom I'm convinced were placed in my life by fate just to keep things interesting. To my extended family, whose unwavering love and support have been the bedrock of my life: you are my roots and my wings.

To my amazing children, whom I adore, and to my stepchildren, their spouses, and their beautiful families—thank you for being my most profound teachers in patience, growth, and the kind of love that doesn't blink when life throws curveballs. You've shown me that resilience isn't loud; it lives in the quiet grace of everyday choices, in the way love shows up even when it's tired. You are living proof that wisdom isn't confined to pages; it often arrives wrapped in belly laughs, midnight confessions (some of which nearly knocked me off my chair), and the gentle bravery of simply being there.

To my grandchildren—my little old souls wrapped in sneakers and bursts of laughter—you are my daily reminders that joy doesn't need grand gestures. It lives in the tiniest giggle, the stickiest hug, and the sweet, unfiltered call of *"Abuela."* You are my heart's playground, my living proof that wonder is always within reach. Watching you grow is like witnessing magic unfold in slow motion, and I am endlessly grateful to walk beside you in this beautiful, messy, love-soaked story.

To my partner—my travel buddy, my sounding board, my co-pilot in this wild ride called life—what a journey it has been. I'm honored to have you beside me, even when I forget where I put my cell phone, and I'm actually talking on it (yes, more than once). You are a truly wonderful human being, and I feel incredibly lucky to share this life with you. Your presence makes the ordinary feel extraordinary, and your love is the compass that keeps me grounded, even when my GPS and my brain go rogue. Thank you, too, for gifting me with your beautiful family.

To my incredible girlfriends, my soul sistahs and brothers, my coworkers who became family, and my brilliant Mastermind crew—you've danced with me through joy, anchored me through storms, lifted me higher than I ever imagined, and yes, occasionally interrupted my Oscar-worthy meltdowns with wisdom and truth. My life would be a completely different story without you in it. Let's just say I chose exceptionally well—and I know how blessed I am because of it. Your presence has been one of life's greatest gifts, and I carry that gratitude with me every single day.

To my teachers, who've shaped my path, inspired my journey, and lovingly kept me in check when I wandered off course, you were the steady hands that helped me find my footing, the gentle voices that reminded me of my worth, and the fierce advocates who saw potential even when I couldn't. Your lessons reached far beyond the classroom, into the corners of my character and the heartbeat of my hope. For every moment you chose patience over frustration, encouragement over critique, and compassion over convenience, I thank you. You didn't just teach me, you truly believed in me and always pushed me to be a better person, and that made all the difference in my life.

To my colleagues and business partners, your collaboration and support have added depth and sparkle to my professional life. I couldn't have done it without you, and I've truly loved every minute of our journey together.

And to my students and clients, thank you. Your curiosity, enthusiasm, and yes, even the occasional eye roll, reminded me daily that learning is a two-way street. You've taught me just as much as I ever hoped to teach you. Each of you has shaped my path in ways big and small, and I'm endlessly grateful for the role you've played in my life.

The love I carry in my heart is stitched together from every lesson, every laugh, and every connection. It is truly a tapestry of love. What a ride. What a blessing. Thank you for inspiring me and for being part of this beautifully chaotic, soul-stretching, laughter-filled journey.

A
ACCEPT DIFFERENCES

Accepting differences isn't just a nice idea—it's essential if you want peace, harmony, and real connection in your life, especially if we want a world where family game nights don't end in food fights, playlists don't spark debates, and political views don't ruin brunch. Every person is a walking blend of experiences, beliefs, and quirks, basically, a human trail mix. And sure, not every ingredient will be your favorite, but the mix? That's what makes life flavorful.

Some folks bring the sweet: compassion, humor, unexpected kindness. Others bring the crunch: boundaries, bold opinions, spicy ideas. There's the occasional raisin of unresolved trauma, the nutty burst of creativity, and the salty wisdom of someone who's weathered a few storms and still shows up with snacks.

Want more flavor? Add your own curiosity, forgiveness, a dash of silliness, and a generous scoop of "I don't have to fix this to love it." Sprinkle in empathy like cinnamon; it warms everything. Toss in some laughter, the kind that snorts out of your nose when you least expect it. And don't forget the dried mango of mystery: the part of someone you'll never fully understand, but that keeps you coming back for more.

The goal isn't to sort the mix, it's to savor it. Because when we stop trying to pick out the pieces we don't like and start appreciating the whole blend, we get a taste of real connection. Accepting differences doesn't mean you have to like every flavor. It means having enough respect to let others be who they are without trying to repackage them into your comfort zone. You don't have to become it. You don't have to endorse it. You just have to let it be and move on with grace.

Why is this so important? Because accepting differences is the foundation of emotional maturity, social harmony, and personal growth. It's how we learn from each other, how we stretch beyond our own biases, and how we build communities that are resilient, inclusive, and real. Without it, we shrink into echo chambers. With it, we expand into possibility.

Diversity of thought, background, and personality is what fuels innovation, empathy, and growth. When we embrace differences, we stretch our perspectives, challenge our assumptions, and expand our capacity to love. It's how we build bridges instead of walls, and how we turn misunderstandings into meaningful dialogue.

Imagine the world we'd live in if we all did that. Less judgment, more curiosity. Fewer arguments, more understanding. It's not about agreeing on everything; it's about agreeing that everyone deserves dignity and the right to their own opinion. Meaningful relationships don't need matching worldviews; they thrive on mutual respect and the occasional, "Huh, I never thought of it like that."

Letting go of the need to be right isn't surrender; it's an open invitation to real conversation (and hopefully a laugh or two). Agreeing to disagree? That's a hidden talent.

If something works for you, fantastic, congratulations. Truly. But that doesn't mean it's the magic formula for everyone else. We're all wired differently, and that's okay. The real challenge is allowing others to be who they are without trying to convert them to your way of thinking.

Trying to convince someone that your way is the only way? That's a fast track to unnecessary arguments. And arguments rarely solve anything. They just multiply. It's like trying to put out a fire with gasoline and a megaphone: loud, messy, and completely ineffective.

Instead of pointing fingers (because let's be honest, the rest of your fingers are pointing right back at you), try pointing toward a solution, or better yet, a few. One of my favorite teachers always said, "Find at least four solutions to any problem." Why four? Because the first one is usually reactive, the second is practical, the third is creative, and the fourth might just be the magical solution. The point is, when you shift from blame to brainstorming, you open the door to collaboration, connection, and maybe even a little joy.

Collaboration isn't just a strategy; it's a love language. It says, "I see you, even if I don't always agree with you." And when we stop trying to win and start trying to understand, we don't just coexist —we create something better together.

฿

BE KIND

Kindness is a daily decision, like choosing your clothes, but with way more emotional impact and zero risk of clashing patterns. It starts with how you talk to yourself. If your inner voice sounds like a grumpy drill sergeant who's had too much coffee and not enough hugs, it's time for a rebrand. Try swapping "Ugh, I messed up again" with "Okay, not ideal, but I'm learning, and I'm still awesome." Bonus points if you say it like you're accepting an award for Most Improved Human.

And today, right before I sat down to write this, I got a real-life reminder of how powerful kindness can be. I went to pick up food and had to wait an extra fifteen minutes. The place was packed, like sardines-in-a-can packed, and while most people were ordering lunch, I was trying to place a catering order (because apparently I enjoy being the logistical curveball). I asked for help and was told the lady at the register would be with me soon, but "soon" kept getting bumped by "just one more customer." I could've gotten annoyed, started crafting a dramatic internal monologue about being ignored, maybe thrown in a sigh or two for flair. But instead, I decided to breathe.

I saw how busy she was. I had a little extra time, so why rush? When she finally got to me, she looked like she'd just run an emotional marathon, visibly shaken, almost in tears. Turns out, she'd been treated poorly by several customers and was completely overwhelmed. Just my calm presence and a simple "Don't worry, I understand" flipped the switch. Her whole demeanor changed. She thanked me profusely and said I'd changed her day. I left her with a wish that she'd have a better one, and she replied, "I already did, because I spoke to you."

Now, I'm not saying I'm always this Zen. Some days I'm one spilled coffee away from a full-blown existential crisis. But today, I made a different choice. I didn't get upset, and that was good for me. Because if I had, I might've missed out on what turned into a genuinely sweet moment.

Kindness is contagious (in a good way), like yawning, but with better branding and actual emotional benefits. A gentle word, a thoughtful gesture, or simply listening without checking your phone every three seconds can leave a lasting impression. People might forget what you said, but they'll remember how you made them feel, especially if you made them feel seen, heard, or like they weren't just background characters in your personal sitcom. And here's the kicker: kindness pays dividends. Not in cash (sorry), but in connection, trust, and the kind of good vibes that make life feel less like a Monday morning and more like a Friday afternoon at five o'clock.

Compliment someone's shoes. Hold the elevator. Let someone merge in traffic without muttering curses under your breath. These tiny acts ripple outward, creating warmth, healing, and maybe even a better day for someone who didn't know they needed it. Kindness also boosts your own well-being. Studies show it lowers stress, strengthens your immune system, and even improves heart health. It's like a wellness supplement you don't have to swallow. You just sprinkle it into your day and watch the benefits unfold. A tiny shift in intention can spark big change. Be patient and kind with yourself first, because once you master that, you'll naturally extend the same grace to others. And let's be honest, the world could use a little more grace and a little less grumpy.

And yes, be kind even if someone isn't. Because when you stroll up to the pearly gates of heaven, God's not going to pull out a scoreboard and say, "Well, they were rude first, so you were totally justified." Nope. He's going to care about what kind of human you were, how kind, how compassionate, how willing you were to rise above the petty stuff. So be the bigger person. Be kind to the unkind. Not because they deserve it, but because you do.

Choose warmth. Choose empathy. Choose kindness. Be gentle with your journey and generous with your heart. After all, kindness isn't just a virtue; it's a superpower disguised as everyday decency.

C

CHOICES

Life is basically a giant choose-your-own-adventure book, except you don't get to peek ahead, and there's no "go back to page 12" option. From deciding whether to eat avocado toast or eggs and ham for breakfast to choosing a career, a partner, or whether to finally start flossing, every choice we make adds a new thread to the wild, colorful tapestry of our lives. Some threads are silk. Some are spaghetti. Some are tangled in glitter. And yes, some are a little frayed. But it's all part of the masterpiece.

The beauty of choice? It's like having a remote control for your own life. You get to pause, reflect, and mentally rewind (no actual time travel, sorry), and switch channels when things get weird. But here's the catch: many of us were raised to believe choices are binary: right or wrong, A or B, yes or no, chocolate or vanilla. But life isn't a vending machine. It's more like a buffet with mystery sauces and surprise desserts. You've got options. So many options. All you need is a curious mind and an open heart, and both are conveniently free and require no subscription.

Choice is power. It's how we reclaim our birthright, rewrite our narratives, and steer our stories in new directions. It's the difference between reacting and responding, between drifting and deciding. Every time you make a conscious choice, you're saying, "I'm here. I matter. I get to shape this."

And here's something we often forget: having choices is a blessing. Not everyone gets that luxury. Some people live in circumstances where options are limited or nonexistent. So, if you're lucky enough to choose your path, your breakfast, your beliefs, your boundaries, don't take it for granted. Use that freedom with intention. Use it to grow, to connect, to uplift. Your choices shape not just your life, but the lives around you.

Feeling overwhelmed by all the possibilities? Totally normal. The fear of making the "wrong" choice can freeze us faster than a Zoom call with bad Wi-Fi. But spoiler alert: there's no universal right answer. Every decision teaches you something, whether it's "I'm brilliant" or "Well, that was a spicy disaster." Mistakes aren't failures; they're plot twists. And plot twists make stories interesting.

Making mistakes isn't just inevitable; it's essential for human growth. It's how we learn, recalibrate, and sometimes discover a better way we never would've seen otherwise. Mistakes? Oh, they'll happen. You're human, not a flawless spreadsheet. When you slip up, skip the self-punishment montage. Haven't you done that enough? Think of mistakes as emotional breadcrumbs leading you toward deeper wisdom.

So, when life throws you a dilemma, don't panic. Breathe. Get quiet. Channel your inner detective. Ask yourself, "What else is possible? How else can I approach this?" The more options you explore, the more empowered you become. You're not a tree rooted and stuck; you're just standing at a crossroads with a map, a flashlight, and a curious mind. Take the first step and go explore.

Take Thomas Edison. The guy tried over 1,200 times to invent the light bulb. That's not failure, that's commitment. If he'd quit after attempt thirty-seven, we'd all be sitting in the dark, bumping into furniture and blaming the dog. Or in my case, my partner (not always, but mostly). But Edison chose to keep going, and every try brought him insight, determination, and progress. Each time you try something different, it adds another color to the tapestry of your life. Repeating the same thing won't lead to new results, so shake things up and take a step forward, even if it feels weird. Especially if it feels weird. That's where break-throughs are born and comfort zones get left behind.

In the end, choices are what make us active participants in our own lives, not just passengers in a derailed train holding on for dear life. So, celebrate your freedom to choose. Be bold. Be curious. Be grateful. And if you mess up? Laugh, learn, and try a different route. After all, even the best plans take unexpected turns, and that's usually where the magic sneaks in.

D

DON'T TAKE THINGS
PERSONALLY AND DON'T ASSUME

Taking things personally is like boarding a flight straight into emotional turbulence: no ticket, no warning, just vibes. It's your brain throwing a glittery tantrum: loud, dramatic, and dressed like it's trying out for Broadway. Classic human behavior, right alongside overthinking and convincing yourself that a headache means you've contracted a rare disease. But let's be real, it's exhausting. You end up starring in imaginary arguments, rehearsing comebacks for conversations that never happened, and spiraling into soap-opera-level drama that plays on loop in your head.

So why do we take things personally? Because at our core, we're wired for connection. We want to feel acknowledged, understood, and valued. When someone rolls their eyes, skips our message, or sends off strange energy, it doesn't just sting; it echoes. It taps into a deeper archive of moments where we've felt overlooked or dismissed.

Think of it like emotional buildup. Every cold glance, unanswered message, or awkward silence adds a drop to the cup. Most days, we carry that cup as if we were walking on a tightrope. But then someone sighs too sharply or forgets a simple "thank you," and suddenly, spill. Not because of that one moment, but because the cup was already full of past experiences.

And when that cup spills, our minds—the master storytellers that they are—turn it into a full-blown saga. One weird interaction becomes, "They hate me. I'm annoying. I should just disappear." Sprinkle in some insecurity, stir with overthinking, and suddenly you're in a courtroom drama where your self-worth is on trial and the judge is your inner critic.

But here's the twist: most people aren't plotting your downfall. They're just trying to survive their own chaos. That snippy tone? Probably stress. That short reply? Maybe they just got bad news. That silence? Could be they're lost in thought or knee-deep in laundry. Nine times out of ten, it's not about you.

So, when your brain starts spinning stories that shrink your confidence, hit pause. Ask yourself, "Is this really about me, or am I writing fiction? What actual evidence do I have that this is personal?"

These questions aren't just clever, they're clarity tools. They help you step out of the fog and into truth. Most of the time, the drama in our heads is louder than reality. Challenge the narrative, and you make room for peace, perspective, and a little self-compassion.

Not taking things personally isn't weakness; it's emotional armor. It protects your energy, your peace, and your ability to respond with love instead of reacting out of fear. When you stop absorbing every interaction like it's a personal attack, you break free from the exhausting loop of self-blame and imaginary conflict. It's not about being indifferent; it's about being wise.

Now let's talk assumptions. They're sneaky little gremlins. "They didn't reply because they're mad at me." Or maybe they're in the shower. Or chasing a raccoon out of their garage. Or just forgot. Assumptions create problems that don't exist, while curiosity builds bridges. Instead of jumping to conclusions, ask, clarify. You'd be surprised how many plot twists vanish with a simple, "Hey, what did you mean by that?"

And if your brain insists on making up stories, at least make them fun. Assume they're rescuing a kitten, winning a dance-off, or deep in conversation with their toaster about the meaning of life. Assume they love you and they're just temporarily trapped in a whirlwind of adulting. If you're going to write fiction, make it a comedy, not a tragedy. Assume grace. Assume good intent. It costs nothing and saves you from carrying pain that was never yours to begin with.

Now, let's zoom out and let's look at things a different way. People are distracted. They've got bills, heartbreaks, deadlines, and maybe a toddler who just flushed their iPhone. When someone snaps or acts like a human thundercloud, it's usually their storm, not yours. They didn't wake up with a mission to throw off your groove, so don't get caught in their weather. You're not the forecast, the fixer, or the emotional sponge. Slip on your metaphorical raincoat, grab those fabulous water shoes, and cruise through the storm like a flamingo on roller skates, graceful, slightly chaotic, but absolutely refusing to fall over.

I can't emphasize enough that before you react … pause … breathe. You can't make wise choices when you're emotionally charged like a lightning bolt, ready to zap the next unsuspecting soul. Channel your inner calm commander, the one who's seen it all and still chooses grace. Try empathy. Try compassion. Responding with kindness isn't just noble; it's emotional kung fu.

Give others the grace you'd want on your worst day and keep it moving like the emotionally evolved legend you are.

Life is too short to take everything personally or to star in your own mental telenovela, complete with imaginary betrayals and a soundtrack only you can hear. Flip the script. And instead of assuming someone's out to wreck your mood, try assuming they're just deep in the chaos of being human. Maybe they're battling inbox overload, trying to remember if they fed the dog, or emotionally recovering from stepping on a Lego. Life is messy. People are messier. So, before you absorb their weird energy, imagine they're just barely holding it together with caffeine and duct tape.

You deserve a better storyline. After all, you really don't know what is happening behind the scenes, and you really don't need to. Does that make you different? Absolutely. And thank goodness for that. You're choosing peace over chaos, for yourself and for the people lucky enough to know you. So next time someone's rude, weird, or just plain confusing, don't spiral.

Smile.

Breathe.

Strut away like the main character you are. You've got better things to do than audition for a role in your own mental rerun.

E

EMBRACE EMOTIONAL AWARENESS

Feelings sometimes feel like the wild ride you didn't sign up for but are already on, but there is one simple truth: recognizing and naming your emotions is like finally reading the instruction manual for your own brain. Without it, you're just winging it, like emotionally freestyling through life, wondering why you keep ending up in Meltdown Meadows or Funky Flats. But once you start identifying what you're feeling, "Oh hey, that's anxiety again," you unlock the first step toward healing: clear communication, and making decisions that don't involve rage-texting your ex or impulse-buying ten pairs of shoes (guilty as charged).

Now, let's talk about honoring those feelings. Yes, honoring. Not stuffing them into your mental junk drawer labeled "Later." See, if you don't acknowledge and honor your feelings, you usually bottle them up like a can of sardines—except this time we are storing them in the body, which creates dis-ease. Those sneaky feelings will come out in some way, so let's learn to release them in healthier ways. Honoring your emotions is like giving your inner world a spa day. Feeling anxious? Great! That means your body's trying to tell you something. Listen to it. Don't ghost your own nervous system.

Here's what you do: First, make sure you are in a safe place. Look around and start naming things like you're hosting a toddler's YouTube channel. "Lamp. Couch. Weird sock. Plant I forgot to water." This grounds you. Then feel your body, yes, that glorious suit, supported by whatever it is touching. Chair? Feet on the floor? Your dog? It doesn't matter. You're supported. You are not flying off in space with no gravity. Now breathe. Deeply. Like you're trying to impress a yoga instructor. Imagine your breath as a glowing orb traveling in and out of your body, bringing in calm and kicking anxiety to the curb like a bad blind date.

Feeling Angry? Good. That means you are alive. But don't let it simmer like emotional chili until it explodes all over your kitchen. And here's the kicker: own it. Your anger is yours. It's not your partner's fault, your kid's fault, or the barista's fault for spelling your name wrong for the fifth time. When your feelings get activated, it's not a cue to launch a blame parade. It's a cue to pause and say, "Whoa, something in me is lit up right now." That's emotional maturity, baby.

Instead of pointing fingers, try pointing inward (gently, not in a self-blaming way). Ask yourself, "What button just got pushed?" Then release it safely. Scream into your hand like you're in a horror movie. Punch a pillow like it owes you rent. Take a kickboxing class and pretend the punching bag is your last passive-aggressive group text. Or throw a ball against the wall repeatedly while yelling, "I am angry because …" It's wildly satisfying and way cheaper than therapy or bail.

Feeling sad? Cry. Cry like you just watched a dog reunion video. Cry like your favorite show got canceled. Cry like your avocado betrayed you by going bad overnight. Crying is a superpower. It's emotional detox. I'm not saying cry in the middle of a board meeting (unless it's really called for), but don't shame yourself for needing to release. Tears are your soul's way of saying, "I'm doing spring cleaning." Tears are soul cleansing. Tears are gifts.

Bottom line: feelings aren't the enemy. They're messengers. Sometimes they show up dressed as anxiety, anger, or sadness, but they're all trying to help you heal, grow, and not explode at the grocery store. So, honor them. Feel them. And maybe keep a pillow nearby just in case.

F

FORGIVE AND APOLOGIZE

Forgiveness is the emotional detox you didn't know you were overdue for. It's not about pretending the hurt never happened; it's about evicting the emotional clutter that's been squatting in your mental space, eating your snacks, and rewinding the worst scenes of a low-rated movie. Forgiving others doesn't hand them a golden ticket; it hands you a moment of peace. You're not saying, "It's fine." You're saying, "I'm done dragging this emotional suitcase with one busted wheel through every airport in the world."

Now, forgiving yourself? That's the boss level. It's looking at your past missteps, giving yourself a compassionate nod, and saying, "Well, that was awkward, but I learned something!" Self-forgiveness doesn't rewrite history; it keeps your future on track. No more emotional detours through Shame Street and Blame Boulevard. That shame and blame don't even belong to you. They're emotional hand-me-downs passed along by parents, teachers, exes, society, or that one friend who thinks sarcasm is a personality. You've been carrying them like a backpack full of bricks, wondering why your emotional posture hurts. But guess what? You can drop it. It's the shift from being haunted to being humbled, the shift from "What's wrong with me?" to "What happened to me?" And that shift? It's powerful. It's liberating. It's like finally realizing the haunted house was just your old beliefs wearing a sheet and yelling "boo."

And when you mess up—and let's be real—we all do, apologize. No need for dramatic monologues or interpretive dance. Just a sincere, "I'm sorry if that hurt you. That wasn't my intention." Boom. That's clarity, kindness, and zero emotional acrobatics. You're not begging for forgiveness; you're simply acknowledging someone's experience. It's like emotional Febreze, it clears the air with no awkward residue.

Forgiveness isn't weakness: it's strength disguised as grace, and it sets you free. It's the courageous choice to say, "I'm choosing healing over harboring." And here's the magic: the more you lean into it, the lighter you become. Like you finally unpacked a suitcase full of grudges and made space for joy, peace, and maybe even a few snacks for the road ahead.

Because in the end, forgiveness isn't about forgetting; it's about freeing. And apologies? They're tiny bridges built with honesty, leading us back to connection. So go ahead, clean the emotional house, toss out the guilt confetti, and make room for something better and healthier. You deserve it.

G

GOLDEN RULE

The Golden Rule, "Do unto others as you would have them do unto you," isn't just for kindergarteners or fortune cookies; it's basically the cheat code for being emotionally evolved. You possess the ability to validate someone's feelings without spiraling into shame or defensiveness. It's not about guilt, it's about grace.

Before you act, ask yourself, "Would I be cool with this if the roles were reversed?" If the answer is "nope," maybe rethink that move. Respect isn't a one-way street. If you want to be respected, start by giving respect. And if you hate being interrupted mid-sentence (who doesn't?), don't be the person who jumps in like they're on a game show buzzer. Listening—actual deep listening—is a power move that says, "I care about what you're saying."

Helping others is always a good idea, but skip the mind-reading. Instead of guessing what someone needs, just ask, "How can I help?" It's respectful, effective, and way less awkward than showing up with a casserole when they needed a ride to the airport.

Living by the Golden Rule means creating a vibe where everyone feels seen, heard, and not secretly judged for their weird coffee order. It's about choosing empathy over ego, curiosity over control, and kindness over being "right." Your compassion can spark a ripple effect—like emotional dominoes, but with hugs, high-fives, and maybe a few healing tears.

And don't forget that the Golden Rule applies to you, too. Treat yourself like someone you actually like. Be kind. Be forgiving. Be the friend who says, "You're doing great, even if today was a bit of a mess." Self-compassion isn't selfish; it is selfless. It is fuel for being awesome to others. Because when you honor your own humanity, you naturally extend that honor to everyone else.

And if you're reading this book, I think you're pretty darn awesome. In fact, you might just be the most awesome person you know. So go ahead, live golden.

H

HOUSECLEANING FOR THE SOUL

Housecleaning for the soul isn't just about sweeping out shame and resentment; it's about tackling the chaos in your physical space that's silently screaming, "I'm overwhelmed!" That pile of unopened mail? Emotional clutter in envelope form. The drawer full of tangled chargers from 2009? Symbolic of your tangled thoughts. That one sock with no mate? A metaphor for your unresolved feelings about Chad from accounting.

Decluttering isn't just tidying up; it is free therapy with a huge trash bag. It's preparing for the future by making your space easier to manage and your mind less likely to spiral when you can't find your keys.

Start with the emotional junk drawer, the one in your head stuffed with "I should've said, blah, blah, blah" and "Why did I do that?" moments. Toss them. You don't need to relive that awkward moment from three years ago. If it still haunts you, light a candle, whisper "I release you," and move on. Then tackle your actual junk drawer. If you haven't used that mystery key in the last decade, it's probably not the key to your destiny. My rule:

If it hasn't served you in six months, let it go. Unless it's ice cream. Ice cream always gets a pass.

Resentment clings like pet hair to your emotional furniture. It is subtle at first, then suddenly you're coughing up a metaphorical furball. Holding grudges is like keeping expired yogurt in the fridge; it's not helping anyone, and eventually, it starts to smell. Toss it before it curdles your vibe. Why on earth are you holding onto that?

Now simplify. Life doesn't need to be a juggling act of stuff, schedules, and self-doubt. Clear your calendar of obligations that drain you. Donate clothes that whisper, "Someday I'll fit into you again," and instead wear things that shout, "I'm fabulous now." Create space, both physically and emotionally, for what truly matters: peace, joy, and maybe a cozy reading nook with zero guilt and one very fluffy blanket.

Finally, open the windows of your heart and your home. Let in fresh air, literally and metaphorically. Emotional housecleaning isn't about perfection; it's about making space for clarity, kindness, and the kind of self-love that doesn't require a scented candle (but hey, if you've got one, light it up). And by the way, who wants to spend their time being perfect? Way too much work, plus you already are perfectly imperfect, and that is what makes you unique.

Clean space. Clear mind. Lighter heart. That's the magic. And unlike some of those dated items in your junk drawer, it never goes out of style.

1

IMPECCABLE WORDS: SPEAK LIGHT, NOT LIGHTNING

One of the things in life you have control over is your word. Your word is power, and not the kind that fries circuits and leaves scorch marks, but more like a flashlight in a dark room. It's meant to guide, not blind. Being impeccable with your word means using it like a beam of light: steady, warm, and helpful. You definitely don't want your words to come across as a lightning bolt. Lightning might be dramatic, but it's unpredictable and occasionally sets things on fire. Not ideal for relationships, reputations, or small children.

And hey, if you're one of those people who prides themselves on being "brutally honest," maybe ease up on the brutality. Honesty doesn't have to come with a side of emotional bruising. Your truth is valid, sure, but it's also your truth. Just because it feels true to you doesn't mean it needs to be broadcast like a weather alert, interrupting everyone's peaceful programming.

Sometimes, the most impeccable word is the one you don't say. If you're unsure, zip it. Pause. Reflect. Give your brain a moment to catch up with your mouth. If you're tempted to overshare, bite your tongue (gently, of course). Think of your words like surprise guests: if they show up unannounced and bring drama, it's chaos. But if they arrive with warmth and pie, next-level human kindness.

So, before you unleash your inner truth lightning bolt, ask yourself, "Is this going to help, heal, or horrify?" If it's the third one, maybe save it for your journal or your therapist. Impeccable speech isn't about being perfect; it's about being intentional, kind, and just a little less shocking. Let your words light the way, not short-circuit the room.

J
JOY

Finding your purpose and chasing your passions can be one of life's greatest joys, like discovering that your weird obsession with organizing spice jars is actually one of your favorite pastimes. It's not about having all the answers (spoiler: no one does), it's about tuning into what makes you feel alive. Think back to the moments that spark joy, ease, or that magical feeling when time vanishes and you forget to check your phone. Whether it's a career path, a creative outlet, or a cause that makes your heart do cartwheels, investing time in what you love gives your life direction and a whole lot more color. The only thing standing between you and that joy is a bunch of limiting beliefs that need to be evicted.

And let's be clear: your purpose doesn't have to be grand, flashy, or Instagram-worthy; it just has to feel real to you. Some of the most meaningful paths start not with a trumpet blast, but with a quiet nudge or a curious whisper like, "Hmm, maybe I do want to learn pottery," or "Why does organizing sock drawers feel so satisfying?" (Actually, the organizing part brings me much joy when I get in the mood, which is not too often).

Want to know your soul's purpose? Easy. What makes you giggle, glow, and forget how long you have been doing it? Do more of that. Try new things. Paint badly. Dance weirdly. Write poetry that rhymes "love" with "dove" and feel no shame. Your joy is your compass. So go forth, karmic superstar, and do the things that bring you joy.

If you haven't found your big passion yet, don't panic. Life is basically a giant art project with no instructions and unlimited glitter—a blank canvas and you're the artist with a wild box of crayons. Try a few colors. Smear some paint. Make a glorious mess. Life's not grading you, and it's not handing out trophies at the finish line. It's a winding, wonder-filled adventure, and you've got every right to switch gears, change colors, and make a new masterpiece. Every experience, every awkward misstep, every moment of awe adds color. It's totally okay to explore, pivot, and try things just because they make you smile. And if you're not sure what brings you joy yet, no worries. Go out and explore, experiment, and savor the moment along the way.

Trust in divine timing. You're not behind, you're exactly where you're meant to be, even if it feels like you're wandering through a cosmic IKEA without a map. Each twist and turn holds clues. So, say yes to new adventures, stay curious, and ditch the pressure to define yourself too soon. For some, it might take a lifetime, and that is okay. Just keep on exploring, keep working on your masterpiece, and make every day a new beginning.

Because here's the truth: life isn't about arriving; it's about evolving, laughing, stumbling, and savoring the ride. We're all headed to the same final destination (yep, death of the physical body), so you might as well enjoy the scenery while you're here. Live intentionally and pursue your passions.

K

KARMA

Karma isn't just a poetic idea from ancient wisdom; it's the universe's quiet way of keeping score. Think of it as a spiritual savings account. Every kind act is a deposit. Every petty move? A withdrawal. Smile at someone, deposit. Snap at a barista because your coffee's late, deduction. The universe doesn't miss a beat. It tracks patterns, not just moments.

Kindness ripples outward. It returns in unexpected ways: a peaceful morning, a stranger's help, a door opening when you least expect it. Chaos and cruelty? They come back with tangled strings and emotional invoices. Every time you choose grace over drama, forgive without applause, or resist the urge to escalate, you're feeding your karma account. It's thriving. Maybe it's stretching in the sun, sipping herbal tea, or alphabetizing its blessings. Whatever it's doing, it's glowing.

But when you ghost someone who deserved honesty, or unleash your inner storm on innocent bystanders, your karma account takes a hit. And here's the twist: your thoughts count, too. That silent judgment, that mental eye roll, that internal grudge?

They're tiny withdrawals. The energy you carry, even when unspoken, shapes your spiritual balance.

The goal is simple: keep your karma abundant. Make more deposits than withdrawals. Be the kind of person your karma would write a thank-you note to and invite over for homemade soup.

Now, of course, you are allowed to feel deeply. Cry. Shout. Eat an entire pizza while watching documentaries that make you question everything. Then light a candle and breathe like you've got nowhere to be but here. Just don't let someone else's bitterness turn you into a karma fugitive. You're free to walk away, skip out, or glide from the chaos like you're starring in your own silent film.

If someone throws negativity your way, let it fall flat like a joke with no punchline. Your energy is too valuable to be tangled in someone else's unresolved mess. Let them wrestle with their own karma while yours wears a velvet robe and hums a tune that feels like home.

If the gossip starts swirling, let it swirl. Let them speculate, analyze, and narrate your life like they've got a backstage pass. Good luck to them because every word they toss into the rumor mill is their karma piggy bank throwing coins into the wind like it's raining money. That's their spiritual savings draining itself for sport. Meanwhile, you stay grounded. Don't join the circus. You don't owe anyone your peace, your time, or your emotional bandwidth. Trying to change someone's mind when they've already decided who you are is like teaching a fish to ride a bicycle; it's pointless, exhausting, and a waste of your brilliance.

Your energy isn't a giveaway item. Stop handing it out like promotional pens at a trade show. Let them be wrong about you. That's their burden to carry. Approval is overrated. Joy is wildly underrated. Choosing yourself is like stepping into sunlight after months of shadow, unexpected, warm, and absolutely necessary.

When something or someone isn't meant for you, release it like leftovers past their prime. You're making space for blessings that don't need preservatives. Just like baking bread, there's no need to rush the rise. You're becoming the kind of person who dances in the kitchen simply because the toast landed butter-side up.

And if you slip, say something you regret, think something bitter, act from a place of fear, it's not the end. Karma isn't about perfection: it's about intention. You can repair the balance. Apologize. Reflect. Choose better next time. Even a quiet moment of self-awareness is a deposit. A sincere "I'm sorry," a shift in perspective, a decision to grow—that's spiritual wealth in motion.

Karma doesn't always pay out instantly. Sometimes it shows up in this lifetime, and sometimes it takes a few more rotations around the sun. But rest assured, the universe never forgets a deposit or a debt.

So, keep making deposits. Laugh often. Choose grace. And know that the universe isn't just watching, it's nodding in approval while your karma account grows interest: one kind act, one deep breath, one moment of clarity at a time. One day, that account will be so full it'll need a ledger, a vault, and maybe a tiny pair of sunglasses to handle all that spiritual wealth.

L
LOVE

I've come to realize that the secret to happiness, the kind that fills your soul and makes life feel like a warm hug from the universe, is surprisingly simple: love. And it all begins with loving yourself. Not in a cliché, Instagram-caption kind of way, but in a real, daily practice kind of way. Loving yourself means showing up for you, and cheering yourself on like a one-person hype squad, even when you accidentally wear mismatched shoes. (Been there, at least they were both the same brand.) It's about forgiving the awkward moments, celebrating the small wins like getting out of bed when gravity feels extra aggressive, and recognizing that you are a majestic, slightly chaotic masterpiece. Perfection is a myth. Real growth happens when you embrace your quirks and wear them like a crown made of glitter and good intentions.

Self-love isn't all bubble baths and sticky notes on mirrors, although I'm a fan of both. It sneaks in during those quiet, unfiltered moments when you realize, "Wait a minute … I'm breathing. That's free. That's amazing." Your body's out here blinking, walking, digesting tacos, and you didn't even have to reboot it this morning. That's magic.

Sometimes I'll stare at the sky like I'm waiting for it to wink back. The clouds are just floating around like they own the place, the trees are doing their leafy thing, standing tall and throwing shade like nature's sass queens, and the sun shows up every day with perfect attendance. The moon's pulling tides like it's casually flexing, and I'm just here, part of this cosmic group project called life. And the wildest part? It's all free. All you have to do is pause, breathe, and look around.

And while you're looking around, don't forget the little things. Your iPhone that somehow knows your face even when you look like a confused potato. Your computer that connects you to the world (and memes). Your job, even if it's just for the snacks in the break room. Your clothes that keep you warm and legally acceptable in public. Clean water. Food in the fridge. The friend who always shows up. The dog that loses its mind when you return from a thirty-second trip to the mailbox. These are life's everyday miracles. Give them a standing ovation.

If you have grandchildren or nieces or nephews or a friend's kid, savor the joy of seeing life through their eyes, wide with wonder, innocent, and bursting with daily miracles. They'll remind you that magic isn't just real, it's everywhere, from bugs on the sidewalk to bedtime stories that somehow require five plot twists and a dragon.

Now, not every single day sparkles. Some days feel like soggy cereal. But that's okay. Tomorrow is a fresh start, a clean slate, a new episode in the series called *You*. And on those off days, love yourself harder. Not because you earned it, but because you deserve it, especially when you feel like you don't.

When you treat yourself like your favorite person, something wild happens: loving others becomes easier, lighter, and way more fun. Life starts to feel like a cosmic block party, and remember: you attract what you radiate. You'll swipe left on chaos, ghost-energy vampires, and block anything that threatens your peace. Your joy expands, your standards rise, and suddenly life feels less like a grind and more like a feel-good movie where your coffee's always the perfect temperature, your phone battery magically stays at 100%, and your favorite song plays every time you walk into a room like you've got your own theme music.

And here's the real magic: when you do everything from a place of love, regardless of what anyone else does, you become untouchable in the best way. Your peace isn't up for negotiation. Your kindness isn't conditional. You love because it's who you are, not because someone earned it. That kind of love is power-ful. It's the kind that transforms rooms, softens hearts, and rewrites stories.

And healing? Real healing doesn't come from overthinking or endless talking; it comes from a heart-centered space. When you drop into love, into compassion, into presence, your soul begins to mend in ways logic can't touch. You don't have to solve every-thing. Sometimes you just have to feel it, breathe through it, and let love do the heavy lifting.

Now picture this: the most important person in your life is coming over for dinner. You'd scrub the floors like Cinderella, light candles, fluff pillows, maybe even iron napkins. (I did that once, still recovering.) But what if You were that person? What if you treated yourself with that same reverence? Roll out the red carpet for your own soul. Be the star of your story, the main character with paparazzi-dodging charm and Oscar-worthy presence. Even if it's leftovers on a Tuesday, make it a cele-bration.

And while you're loving yourself, extend that grace to others. People are delightfully weird. They'll borrow your charger and never return it, talk through the best part of the movie, and somehow forget turn signals exist. Love them anyway. When you're grounded in self-love, you laugh more, judge less, and even your grumpy neighbor starts to seem oddly lovable.

And if someone comes along who makes your heart do cartwheels and wraps your soul in a warm burrito of joy, hold on tight. Love them boldly. Build something beautiful. That kind of connection is rare and delicious, like finding a $100 bill in your coat pocket unexpectedly on laundry day.

But if you're in a relationship where you're being treated like a background character in someone else's drama, it's time to exit stage left. Not necessarily with fireworks (unless you're feeling theatrical), but with quiet strength and a playlist that screams, "I choose peace." Loving yourself means knowing when to walk away. You deserve to be seen, valued, and cherished, not just tolerated.

So, love deeply. Laugh loudly. Be grateful for everything—the big stuff, the little stuff, and the weird stuff in between. You're not just worthy of love. You are love. You're the living, breathing embodiment of it. The perfect frequency. The real deal. Pure vibration of love. That's you.

M
MOURNING

This topic has always touched me deeply. Change used to feel like an unwelcome visitor—unpredictable and uncomfortable. But over time, I've come to see it differently. Change is not something to fear; it is something to embrace. It is the doorway to growth, to renewal, and to unexpected blessings.

Whether it's a new job, a move to a different city, the end of a relationship, or the loss of someone dear, change often brings with it a period of mourning. And mourning, I've learned, is not a straight path. It moves in circles. One moment you may feel angry, the next you are overcome with sadness. Sometimes both emotions arrive together, swirling like a storm. This is normal. This is human. Be patient with yourself. Let the emotions rise and fall. Healing has its own rhythm.

Even the most painful changes can carry hidden gifts. Looking back, I've found gratitude tucked inside every transition, even the ones that felt unbearable. And if you're not feeling thankful right now, that's okay, too. There is no need to judge yourself. We are all doing the best we can.

The death of a loved one—a parent, a friend, a spouse, a child, or a beloved pet—is a sacred kind of grief. You can have deep faith, and I like to think I do, but faith does not erase the ache. You must give yourself permission to grieve. For some, that takes months. For others, years. There is no right timeline. Every soul is unique, and every journey through grief is valid.

I believe we are here on Earth as visitors. We are gathering wisdom, learning lessons, and growing through love and loss. This world may feel like home, but it is temporary. Our true home, I believe, is with God in heaven—a place of peace, joy, and freedom from suffering. Imagine your loved ones there, whole and happy. It is a comforting thought, even when our minds resist it. The ego clings to pain, but the soul understands that death is not the end. It is a return.

Still, mourning is necessary. It is sacred. So, allow yourself to feel it all. You can grieve and still laugh. You can miss someone deeply and still find joy in your day. You can be happy that they are in heaven and still ache for their physical presence. That duality is not a contradiction: it's a reflection of love.

And love never dies. It stays. It lingers. It lives in your heart, in your memories, and in the quiet moments when you feel their presence. If you quiet your mind, you may sense them nearby. You may feel their love wrapping around you like a warm blanket.

Now ask yourself this: If your loved one could see your suffering, what would they say? I believe they would tell you to keep going, to live your life. They would say, "I'm okay. You will be too." That is faith. That is love.

So, honor your feelings—every single one. And if the weight feels too heavy, please reach out. There is no shame in asking for help.

Sometimes we all need a hand to hold, a voice to guide us, a reminder that we are not alone.

Here are a few quotes that have helped me through the fog:

- "Don't let one loss become the end of many lives still being lived."
- "Let their passing break your heart, not your spirit."
- "Their death is not meant to be the end of your life too."
- "Grieve deeply, but don't let their death take you with it."
- "Honor their life by continuing yours. Don't let their death become the end of your light."
- "Grieve, remember, love. But don't let their passing become your undoing."
- "They may be gone, but you're still here for a reason. Keep living, for both of you."
- "Let their memory be your strength, not your surrender."
- "Carry them with you, but don't let their absence carry you away."

To everyone carrying the weight of loss, I am so sorry. I hold you in my thoughts and prayers as you move through this season of grief.

N

NATURAL AWAKENING

Natural Awakening is a growing community of people intentionally cultivating awareness, compassion, and inner peace, like emotional gardeners planting seeds of kindness and pulling weeds of judgment. Together, we're creating a society that's more harmonious, awakened, and slightly less likely to yell at strangers in traffic. (Progress!)

And when enough of us start tending our inner gardens, something bigger begins to bloom. That's where the Conscious Collective comes in. It's what happens when personal growth throws a party and invites the whole planet. Think of it as a spiritual group project, but instead of passive-aggressive emails and one person doing all the work, everyone's contributing their own flavor of healing, awareness, and occasional chaos. At its core, it's the belief that personal transformation leads to collective healing. Translation? When you do the inner work, you're basically helping humanity clean up its emotional inbox. On the other hand, when you're acting like a fool, scolding your cat for taking its fifth nap of the day while you haven't even figured out lunch, you're also contributing to the collective. Yes, even your feline envy is part of the cosmic upload. Congrats! You're part of the problem and the solution.

Enter Natural Awakening. It's like your soul finally stretching after a long nap and realizing you've been using your phone's flashlight to look for your phone for years. It's that moment when you realize your thoughts have power, your energy has influence, and your habit of talking to your houseplants might actually be part of your spiritual path. Turns out, they've been your silent gurus all along. Natural Awakening doesn't have to be dramatic like a drumroll at a beauty pageant. It's subtle, like realizing your houseplants have been judging you this whole time and you're finally ready to listen.

At its heart, the Conscious Collective is built on the idea that whatever you do, whatever you think, all gets computed into the mainframe of the universal consciousness, like a giant cosmic chalkboard where everyone's doodles matter. So, when you do your inner work—yes, even the messy kind that involves crying in the car and journaling like your pen is on fire—you are actually helping humanity clean up its emotional inbox. Think of it as spiritual composting: turning your emotional leftovers into fertile ground for growth. Every time you choose compassion over clapback, or presence over panic, you're tossing a kindness boomerang into the ether.

This collective is built on shared values, beliefs, and moral attitudes that unify us. I'm not implying we all think alike. Please, we can't even agree on how to pronounce "acai." Every thought we think, every word we speak, every action we take uploads data into this shared consciousness. So yes, your random epiphanies and 3:00 a.m. journal entries? They matter. Even your shower arguments with imaginary coworkers are getting logged somewhere in the cosmic database.

All your thoughts and actions matter. They're being registered, archived, and possibly backed up on some intergalactic cloud server for future generations to feel, decode, and maybe laugh at. So go ahead, think big, love hard, and argue passionately with your shampoo bottle. The universe is listening, and it's taking notes.

In the spiritual sense, the Conscious Collective loves its mindfulness, meditation, and holistic wellness. It's like the soul's version of a farmer's market: organic, intentional, and slightly overpriced. These tools help us awaken to our true nature and interconnectedness, empowering us to heal emotionally, mentally, and spiritually. And when we heal ourselves, that healing ripples outward, like a group hug that spans continents, minus the awkward silence.

Of course, we're human. We trip over our own egos, binge-watch distractions, and occasionally forget where we put our compassion. But here's the good news: when negativity shows up like an uninvited guest, we don't have to serve it anything. We can choose a better thought. And that choice? It's how we start healing the collective, one mindful moment at a time.

I once heard that the path to enlightenment is no longer than the journey from our head to our heart. But one of my teachers said it's even shorter: just a single thought. That's right, your next brilliant idea could be the spiritual equivalent of a mic drop.

So, let's contribute thoughts that uplift, heal, and inspire. Let's toss new ideas into the collective like glitter bombs of insight, sparkly, surprising, and impossible to vacuum out of the universe. Because, whether we realize it or not, we're all tuning into that shared field, especially children, who absorb our energy like little emotional sponges with zero filter.

Choose your thoughts wisely. They echo further than you think. And who knows? Your next idea might just be the one that shifts the whole vibe or at least gets us one step closer to a world where people stop arguing in the comments section.

40

O

OPEN YOUR MIND

Open your mind by opening a new door to change by walking through it yourself. Don't wait for someone else to hold it open while you rehearse your entrance. Don't stand on the porch of possibility, hoping the wind will blow you in. You've got to be the one who turns the handle, steps through, and says, "Surprise! I brought a surprise." Because change shows up when you do.

Feeling fearful? Good. That's usually the universe's way of saying, "Buckle up, something's about to shift." Sure, change can be scary, but what's even scarier is staying stuck in the same loop, binge-watching your own comfort zone while life keeps evolving without you.

Here's how I see it: if you try, you've got a fifty-fifty shot at success. Not bad odds, especially considering most vending machines are less reliable. But if fear talks you out of even trying? That's a guaranteed 100% miss. No growth, no glory, just a front-row seat to your own potential … still waiting in the wind.

And let's be real: to get what you've never had, you've got to do what you've never done. That might mean waking up earlier, saying no to things that drain you, or finally breaking up with your comfort zone. It's like trying to bake a cake with the same old ingredients and wondering why it still tastes like procrastination. New results require new recipes, and yes, sometimes you'll burn the first batch. That's part of the flavor.

So go ahead and take the leap, make the weird choice, say yes to the thing that makes your stomach do cartwheels. Open your mind to growth. Growth isn't always glamorous. Sometimes it looks like crying in yoga class or Googling "how to be brave" at 2:00 a.m. But every step you take through that door is a declaration: I'm not waiting for change. I am the change. And I brought angelic friends.

And when you open your mind, you open yourself to possibilities that didn't exist before. You might discover a new passion that lights you up from the inside out. You might build a connection with someone who challenges and expands your worldview. You might finally forgive yourself for something you've been carrying for years. You might even realize that the life you've been dreaming of isn't as far away as you thought; it's just been waiting for you to say yes.

Opening your mind isn't about abandoning who you are; it's about becoming more of who you're meant to be. So, stretch, soften, and step forward. The door's already there. All that's left is for you to walk through it.

P

PAUSE

We live in a world that's basically sprinting in high heels, fast-paced, chaotic, and slightly painful. We're constantly on the move, and even when our bodies are still, our minds are doing cartwheels. We scroll through the Internet like it's a second job, check emails like we're waiting for a Nobel Prize notification, and bounce between Instagram, Facebook, WhatsApp, Signal, texts, and whatever other digital circus is performing that day.

Even our toddlers are out here multitasking, snacking, watching cartoons, and somehow managing to FaceTime grandma all at once. The hustle is real. And then we sit there, wide-eyed and frazzled, wondering why we have anxiety. Spoiler alert: it's because our brains haven't had a coffee break since who knows when.

So, here's a wild idea: Pause, like actually pause. Not the kind where you pretend to meditate but secretly plan dinner in your head or mentally redesign your living room. I mean a real, intentional moment of stillness. Breathe like you mean it. Inhale peace, exhale stress. Inhale calm, exhale that weird email from your boss. Let your nervous system take a nap; it deserves it. You deserve it. Our nervous system works best when it is fully rested. It cannot do its best if it is exhausted.

Pausing isn't laziness; it's medicine. It's the reset button your body and brain have been begging you to press. When you pause, your cortisol levels drop, your heart rate slows, and your mind gets a chance to stop spinning like a hamster on a wheel. Your immune system gets a boost, your digestion improves, and your mood gets a little less "doom scroll" and a little more "I've got this."

You don't need a three-hour spa day (though, let's be honest, that is amazing and is definitely my idea of relaxation). Just a few deep breaths can do wonders. Go outside and connect with nature. If you're stuck in an office, keep photos on your desk of whatever brings you joy: puppies, kids, sunsets, or that one vacation where you didn't check your phone every three minutes. Stretch your body. Close your eyes for sixty seconds. Sip your tea like it's a sacred ritual instead of a caffeine delivery system.

Pausing also helps you reconnect with yourself. It's in those quiet moments that you hear your own thoughts, feel your own feelings, and remember that you're more than your to-do list. You're a living, breathing, feeling human, not a productivity machine. And the more you pause, the more you create space for clarity, creativity, and calm to enter.

Bottom line: you're not a robot. You're a beautifully unique human who needs rest. So, give yourself permission to pause. Your soul will send you a thank-you note, your body will throw a mini parade, and your mind might finally stop rehearsing imaginary arguments with your neighbor about recycling bins. Pausing isn't a luxury; it's a lifeline. Take it. You've earned it.

Q

QUESTION YOUR DOUBTS BEFORE YOU QUESTION YOUR DREAMS

Question your doubts before you question your dreams because, let's be real, doubts are like that flaky friend who never replies to your texts but somehow always shows up with unsolicited advice and a bad attitude. They barge in wearing sweatpants, dragging a suitcase full of insecurity, and start redecorating your mental space like they own the place. Meanwhile, your dreams are outside, dressed in style, bouncing like a hyper cheerleader, waving a vision board and yelling, "Pick me! Pick me! I've got plans!"

Now picture this: a cartoon angel and devil perched on your shoulders. The devil's your doubt—tiny, loud, and weirdly obsessed with worst-case scenarios. The angel? That's your dream—glowing, fabulous, and armed with a megaphone. Turn up the angel's volume. Let her sing and shout. And when that little doubt-devil starts whispering nonsense, grab the remote and change the movie reel in your head. Switch from "What if I fail?" to "What if I fly?"

Does this take work? Absolutely. But guess what else takes work? Building mental obstacle courses complete with emotional hurdles, self-doubt tunnels, and a finish line that keeps moving every time you get close. If you're going to put in the effort, why not channel it into something that actually lifts your spirit instead of dragging you through the mud?

Your brain is already working overtime, so might as well give it a better script, a script where you are the hero of the story, not the background character in a terrible soap opera. Do what is best for you. Do what brings you joy. You deserve a starring role in a beautiful movie!

R
RELATIONSHIPS

Are relationships challenging? Oh, absolutely. Being in a relationship is challenging, and not being in a relationship is challenging, too. Choose your challenge. But you know what else is challenging? Running a mile in under ten minutes. So really, it's about choosing your flavor of difficult. Life doesn't promise ease, but it does offer growth. Challenges nudge us to level up, stretch beyond our comfort zones, and keep giving it another shot.

Every person you meet comes bearing gifts, and not the kind you register for at a baby shower, but the kind wrapped in life lessons. And yes, sometimes those gifts feel like getting underwear as a kid for Christmas: awkward, unexpected, and not exactly thrilling. But they're still gifts. Because we're here to learn, to grow, to stumble, and occasionally to cry into a bowl of ice cream at 2:00 a.m. That's the beauty of it. The hard stuff teaches us the good stuff, and every challenge is a doorway to something deeper, wiser, and more real.

Relationships are like enrolling in the most unpredictable class you'll ever take. There are pop quizzes, surprise exams, and the occasional group project where one person does all the emotional heavy lifting. But if you're willing to show up, study each other's quirks, and co-author the syllabus, you'll realize love isn't just a warm fuzzy feeling; it's a skill we can spend a lifetime trying to master. It's communicating like you're delivering a heartfelt acceptance speech at an imaginary awards show for emotional maturity, especially when the conversation involves dishes left in the sink. It's choosing curiosity over criticism, asking, "What made you feel that way?" instead of "Are you seriously mad about this?" It's about listening like your soul's taking notes, summoning lots of patience (the kind that could outlast a DMV line), and laughing, laughing until your belly aches, your mascara runs, and someone snorts. Humor is emotional WD-40; it loosens the tension and keeps the wheels turning.

Apologizing is another underrated superpower. A simple "I'm sorry" can do more than a ten-page text message that reads like a dramatic screenplay about your intentions. You're not admitting to being a villain in a soap opera; you're just acknowledging someone's feelings. It's not about who's right or wrong; it's about creating a space where both people feel safe, seen, and slightly less dramatic.

Now, let's talk about love. It's not about finding someone who completes you like a missing puzzle piece; it's about finding someone who complements your chaos and still wants to build a home with you during thunderstorms. And that whole "relationships are 50/50" myth? Toss it. Real love is 100/100, two people showing up fully, over and over and over again.

Of course, if you're in a relationship where you don't feel safe or respected, you are free to walk away. But don't let "walking away" become your go-to escape route. If there's love, there's usually room to repair. Try therapy. If one therapist feels like a bad first date, try another. And let's normalize something: "I love them, but I'm not in love" is often code for "I've lost touch with my own joy." Being in love starts with you. Lust is the glittery intro, and love is what's left when the lust settles and you're both in sweatpants, figuring out dinner. Don't waste your lifetime looking for someone who completes you. Only you can complete yourself.

True love lives in the little things: the way they make your coffee, the way they show up when you're cranky, the way they remember your weird childhood stories. It's not a fairy tale; it's more like tending an olive tree—slow-growing, deeply rooted, and worth every season.

So be creative. Be weird together. Take on the world like a team of slightly dysfunctional superheroes. Celebrate the ordinary. Grow together. And above all, treat each other like best friends who actually like each other. Because at the end of the day, love isn't just about romance; it's about partnership, playfulness, and showing up, even when you'd rather hide under the covers.

Oh, yes, I don't want to forget trying to make that person think like you, agree with you, or wanting to mold or change that person the way you want. You cannot mold a person. People are like overcooked spaghetti—floppy, unpredictable, and absolutely refusing to stick to the perfect shape you had in mind. Attempting to shape others according to your own expectations will lead to disappointment and lots of failure.

We all come pre-seasoned with ideas, traumas, and unsolicited opinions, and that is what makes us unique. There are no two people alike. I often say, "Thank God there is not another Dania like me." I am pretty sure I would divorce myself.

Try to focus on the positive. Remember the reason you chose each other and take on the motto, "Do I want to be right or do I want to be happy?" And no, you cannot be both all the time, so choose wisely.

S

SIMPLIFY LIFE (BEFORE
LIFE COMPLICATES YOU)

Most of the stress we carry? Honestly, it's like we ordered it ourselves. Instead of extra cheese, we order extra anxiety, hold the peppers. We push to achieve more, do more, be more, and end up like a browser with forty-seven tabs open, one of them playing music, but you can't find which one! Meanwhile, our loved ones are just trying to keep up without getting hit by flying expectations.

Yes, dreams and goals are great. But so is sleep. So is peace. So is not crying in the car because your to-do list is longer than a CVS receipt. Simplifying doesn't mean giving up ambition; it means asking, "Do I really need this, or am I just collecting stress like it's on sale?"

A simpler life isn't boring; it's brilliant. It's choosing experiences over stuff, clarity over clutter, and joy over juggling flaming swords of obligation. And no, I'm not saying you need to live in a tiny house and eat lentils forever (unless you love lentils, then live your best legume life). Want a bigger home or a shinier car? Go for it. Just don't let those things own you. The only thing you'll take from this life is your memories. Not your couch, not your blender, and definitely not your iPhone.

Start small. Declutter a drawer, a corner, a closet, whatever feels doable. You'll be amazed at how clearing physical space clears mental space. It's like your brain finally gets a chance to exhale.

Next, guard your time like it's the last piece of chocolate. Say no to things that drain you. "No" is a complete sentence, and it can be said with a smile and zero guilt. You're not a walking RSVP machine; you're a human being with priorities. Being tired and resentful aren't personality traits; they are cries for help, for boundaries.

If you've got kids, remember that taking care of yourself isn't selfish; it's leadership. You're showing them how to be whole, not just how to be helpful.

Simplify your finances. Budget like a boss. Cut out the stuff that doesn't serve you, like the subscription to that app you forgot existed. You don't need to keep up with anyone else's highlight reel. Life isn't a competition; it's a journey, and you're the CEO of your own peace.

And please, for the love of sanity, reduce screen time. Social media is great for memes and cat videos, but it's also a black hole for your creativity. Instead of scrolling, go for a walk, read something that interests you (maybe even something educational), or call someone who remembers your landline number.

Envision your path, but aim for goals that don't require a cape or a PhD in perfection. Break them down into snackable steps—the kind that don't choke your spirit. Celebrate every mini win like it's a parade in your honor. And when life tosses your plans into a merengue misstep? That's not failure, it's just life whispering, "Time to pivot, darling." And that's where the juicy lessons live.

So, stir the pot. Try the thing. Take the chance. And if fear shows up? Welcome it with a nod, but don't rent it a room in your head. Just let it pass through like a tourist. It's not here to stay; just here to teach.

52

T

TRAUMA

Let's talk about trauma— not the stub-your-toe kind, but the deep emotional kind; the kind that hides in your nervous system like a critter in your attic, making noise at 3:00 a.m. Trauma from the past has a sneaky way of showing up in the present, dressed as anxiety, self-sabotage, or that sudden urge to cancel plans and binge-watch documentaries about ancient civilizations. But here's the truth: just because something happened to you doesn't mean it gets to define you. You are not your trauma. You are not the heartbreak, the betrayal, the silence, the shame, or the storm. You are the one who survived it, and that's worth honoring.

Understanding trauma isn't about blaming yourself or reliving every painful moment; it's about gently turning on the light in the room where you've been storing all the emotional clutter. You don't have to unpack it all at once. You don't need to fix yourself, because you're not broken. You're healing, and healing isn't a straight line; it's more like a dance between progress and naps.

So how do you heal? With compassion, with patience, with the kind of love you'd give a friend who's been through hell and still shows up for you. Start by talking about it with a therapist, a trusted soul, or even your journal. Your truth deserves to be heard, even if your handwriting looks like a cryptic treasure map. Then move your body—not to punish it, but to remind it that it's safe now. Stretch, walk, dance like nobody's watching, and if they are, charge admission. Forgive yourself for the ways you coped when you didn't know better. You were doing your best with what you had. That's not weakness; that's resilience in disguise.

And here's a powerful addition: reconnect with your inner child —that younger version of you who needed safety, love, and validation. Healing often means sitting with that child, listening to their fears, and offering the comfort they never received. Write them letters. Let them draw. Let them play. Let them cry. Let them be seen.

Inner child work isn't about staying stuck in the past; it's about reclaiming the parts of you that were left behind and rewriting the story they were forced to tell. It's about gently challenging the beliefs that the wounded child made about themselves. Beliefs like "I'm not enough," "I'm too much," or "I have to earn love." These were survival thoughts, not truths. And now, as the adult in the room, you get to choose new beliefs rooted in worthiness, safety, and self-compassion.

It's also about recognizing the behavior patterns that the child adopted to feel safe—people-pleasing, perfectionism, shutting down, lashing out—and asking, "Does this still serve me?" You're not betraying your past by changing; you're honoring it by evolving. You're giving that child what they needed all along: someone who sees them, protects them, and loves them unconditionally. This way, you get to gently learn how to re-parent that inner child in a healthy, loving way.

When you do this work, you don't just heal; you transform. You become the safe space you always needed. You become the love you were searching for. And that changes everything.

Most importantly, love yourself through it; not just when you're glowing and grounded, but when you're messy and moody and wearing pajamas that have seen better days. Healing from a heart-centered space means you stop trying to think your way out of pain and start feeling your way into peace. It's softer, slower, deeper, and it works.

You're allowed to be a masterpiece and a work in progress at the same time. So go ahead: cry when you need to, laugh when you can, and keep showing up for yourself like you're the most important person in your life because you are. And the more you heal, the more you help heal the world, one gentle, intentional, wildly courageous step at a time.

U
USE YOUR VOICE

Use your voice, even if it quivers. Your voice is yours. Not borrowed, not leased, not on layaway. It's your divine, occasionally dramatic instrument of truth. Use it.

Sure, there are moments when silence is golden, like when someone's chewing loudly and you're trying not to commit a felony. But, more often than not, what you need is to use your voice and speak. Say what you feel. Say what you think. Say it with love, say it with an eyebrow raised if needed, but say it.

If you're afraid you might say something inappropriate, take a pause before you speak. A couple of deep breaths can give your nervous system a moment to settle and your mind a little space to choose your words with care. You don't have to rush. You don't have to be perfect. You just have to be present. The only way people are going to know what your desires are is if you speak, gently but firmly. You're allowed to be clear. You're allowed to be kind. You're allowed to be both.

Your thoughts and feelings aren't leftovers; they are the main course. They matter. They're valid. They're not up for public vote or committee approval. When you love and value yourself, you become less susceptible to other people's unsolicited opinions, passive-aggressive sighs, or that one aunt who is constantly commenting on your body weight.

And let's be clear: there are many ways to use your voice. You can go full spicy and say, "You're a jerk and I don't like what you did." Or you can take the diplomatic route: "What you just did doesn't sit well with me, so please don't do it again." Either way, you're not bottling it up like an emotional bomb. Emotional bombs can easily detonate inside us, which can then become dis-ease of the body. Let that shit go.

As kids, some of us were taught to hush, to shrink, to nod politely while our souls screamed "Nooooo!" But guess what? You're not a kid anymore. You're the grown-up now. You're the narrator of your own story, not the background hum.

So, speak, sing, whisper, roar. And if you're not quite ready to speak it out loud? That's okay. Write it. Scribble it. Journal it. Let it spill onto the page like emotional confetti. It's healthy, it's healing, and it's yours. Just don't let your truth go stale in the back of the fridge.

Because your voice isn't just sound, it's actual power. And it's time to turn the volume up. Your voice isn't just a tool; it's a bridge, a boundary, a beacon, a gift from God. It's how you honor your heart, how you connect, how you heal. So don't wait until the moment has passed and you're left rehearsing comebacks in the shower like a soap opera. Honor yourself. Release it.

V

VICTIM TRIANGLE

The foundation of codependency. The birthplace of drama. Not the cute rom-com kind, but the full-blown soap opera, complete with emotional cliffhangers and imaginary violins. The Victim Triangle, also known as the Drama Triangle, was gifted to us by Dr. Stephen Karpman in the 1960s and is basically the blueprint for how to turn everyday life into an Academy Award-winning meltdown.

It brilliantly maps out how we learned to tango with drama: unhealthy boundaries, shame and blame, guilt and resentment, and a general lack of personal power served with a splash of inner emotional chaos. It's like a dysfunctional family starter pack: just add water, and unresolved childhood wounds begin to surface.

But hey, once you understand the triangle, you can make it your life's mission to work at staying clear of it, and suddenly, you're not starring in a drama; you're directing a healing.

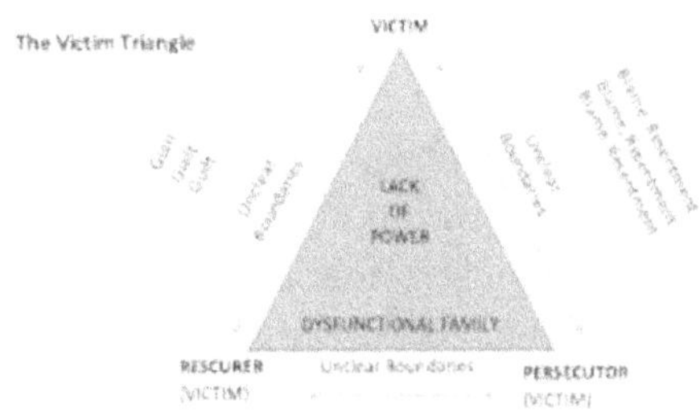

Let's begin with the Rescuer: the Drama Triangle's well-meaning paramedic, sprinting in with a casserole of comfort and a toolkit of unsolicited solutions. Their intentions? Pure. Their boundaries? Probably hanging out with mismatched socks and expired coupons. Rescuers thrive on being indispensable. You'll hear them say, "I've got this," or "You shouldn't face this alone," and the ever-popular, "If not me, then who?" Noble? Yes. Sustainable? Not even close.

They're the ones who show up with snacks, spreadsheets, and a sixth sense for other people's chaos. But while they're busy patching up everyone else's emotional potholes, their own needs get buried under a landslide of neglected self-care. Eventually, the cape feels less heroic and more like Velcro on bare skin— loud, clingy, and difficult to peel off. The exhaustion creeps in. The inbox of other people's problems overflows, and suddenly, the Rescuer is fantasizing about a silent retreat or a nap that lasts until next spring.

And here's where the shift to Victim happens. When the Rescuer's tank runs dry, the Victim energy tiptoes in, not as a new character, but as a subtle change in emotional weather. It's not always loud. Sometimes it's just a sigh that says, "Does anyone even notice?" The triangle isn't about labels; it's about roles we rotate through, often without realizing. Each corner carries a flavor of helplessness, of victimhood, whether it's masked as martyrdom, blame, or burnout.

Picture the multitasking mom juggling errands, refereeing sibling squabbles, and ghostwriting science projects. She started out as the helper, but now she's folding laundry like it's a Shakespearean monologue, muttering, "I guess I'm the only one who cares." She has become the Victim. To all the powerhouse parents out there: you're not a solo act. Pass the baton. Share the load. You're building a community, not running a kingdom.

Then there's the employee who says yes to everything, stays late, and becomes the unofficial office therapist. At first, they're celebrated. Later, they're crying in the supply closet, whispering, "Why does no one notice?" Or the friend who's always available, always listening, until she's emotionally dehydrated and wondering if anyone sees her as more than a sounding board.

And now we arrive at the third role: the Persecutor. This isn't a villain; it's a wounded part of us that flips the script from "I'm overwhelmed" to "Everyone else is the problem." It's not a conscious choice. It's the nervous system staging a coup, hijacked by unresolved junk from the emotional attic. One minute you're seeking empathy, the next you're starring in a courtroom drama, complete with finger-pointing, sarcasm, and resentment.

You might catch yourself delivering "feedback" that really is just judgment in a glittery disguise. Or maybe your eyerolls deserve their own Olympic category (guilty as charged here). It's not cruelty; it's a coping mechanism—a way to reclaim control when everything feels off kilter. But here's the magic trick: pause. Breathe. Whisper to the inner dragon, "I see you. Let's not burn the village today." That moment of awareness can shift everything. A simple moment of pause can reshape the story.

These roles aren't fixed; they're fluid. One moment you're the fixer, the next you're the critic, and suddenly you're the one curled up with a pint of ice cream, wondering how you got here (guilty as charged, too). The triangle isn't a personality test; it's a relational dance we learn early, often without knowing we're enrolled. There is no syllabus, just inherited patterns and emotional reflexes.

Even in traffic, the triangle shows up. You're the victim of bad infrastructure, the persecutor of reckless drivers, and the rescuer, soothing yourself with whatever fast food shows up nearby.

Then comes the inner dialogue: "Why do I always do this?" (Victim), "I have no self-control!" (Persecutor), "I'll fix it tomorrow with a juice cleanse and a vision board." (Rescuer). We even do it with texts. Someone doesn't reply, and suddenly we're abandoned, angry, and inventing a dozen rescue plans that involve zero actual communication.

So how do we exit this emotional merry-go-round? Radical responsibility. That's the off-ramp. It's not about blame; it's about ownership. Your feelings are valid. Your reactions are clues. Your choices are the steering wheel. Anger? That's your inner compass saying, "Something's not right." Don't hand that compass to someone else. Ask it what it's trying to show you. Your feelings are yours to own. No one is responsible for how you feel. You are 100% responsible for how you feel. Own it. Let's be honest: the person who cut you off this morning isn't Mario Andretti gunning for first place. Maybe they made a mistake. Maybe they were rushing to an emergency. Or maybe they just missed their coffee, and their brain's still buffering. But here you are, upset and calling them names that would make your grandmother clutch her pearls.

The truth? You're the one who is angry. That mystery driver? They've probably already forgotten the whole thing and are singing along to bad 80s hits, blissfully unaware they've become the villain in your mental soap opera.

Now let's talk boundaries, the kind that protect your peace, like knowing when to walk away from the domino table before your tío starts slamming tiles and calling everyone "caballo." Boundaries aren't walls; they're filters. They help you decide which games are worth playing and when to fold your hand and exit stage left. Setting boundaries is like installing emotional antivirus software. Because when you know your worth, someone else's opinion is just background noise.

Remember that "No" is a full sentence. It doesn't need a thesis or a pie chart. Before you RSVP to someone else's crisis, ask, "Am I doing this from love, or am I hoping for applause?" Kindness is generous. Rescuing is performative. One nourishes. The other depletes.

When you set boundaries, expect a few grumbles. Let them grumble. It's like switching up the choreography mid-performance. Some folks will trip over their own feet, protest the new moves, and insist the old routine was better. But give it time, they'll either learn the steps or sit out. Either way, you're dancing to a new, healthier rhythm now. Stay the course. Remember, you're not building walls, you're planting flags for healthier connection.

And when someone speaks to you in a way that makes your inner compass spin, pay attention. That shift isn't drama, it's data. It's your intuition whispering, "Something is off." In that moment, you're being invited to choose growth over shrinking, to honor your truth without theatrics. So, take a breath, stand in your center, and say it calmly: "That didn't sit well with me. Please adjust your tone." That is not confrontation, it is calibration. It's how we teach others to meet us in mutual respect. It's how healthier relationships begin.

Every time you choose clarity over chaos, you rewrite the script. You become the director of your own emotional narrative. You are no longer auditioning for approval; you're producing your own show, and it sparkles.

W

WORK HARD AND WORRY LESS

"Work hard and worry less" isn't just a motivational phrase stitched onto a decorative pillow you'd find at your aunt's house, nestled between the plastic-covered couch and the bowl of hard candy no one eats. It is a practical philosophy for navigating life with purpose and peace, and maybe a little less dramatic sighing. Working hard doesn't mean burning yourself out or chasing perfection like a caffeinated squirrel. It means showing up consistently, giving your best effort, and staying committed to growth. It is about taking pride in what you do, whether it is a high-stakes project or just remembering to water the plant you swore wasn't dead yet. Effort compounds over time like interest, except this kind actually pays off in confidence and self-respect.

Here is the thing: doing your best doesn't look the same every day. Some days, your best might be tackling a full to-do list with laser focus and a playlist that makes you feel invincible. Other days, it might mean simply showing up, staying afloat, and not yelling at the printer. If you are sick, your best might be curling up in bed with a blanket and some chicken soup, letting your body heal instead of trying to conquer the world in pajamas.

Effort isn't always about output. Sometimes it is about self-awareness and knowing when to pause. Honoring your limits is part of working hard, too. And no, that doesn't mean you are slacking; it means you are human.

Now, about worrying less. It is not about pretending everything is fine while your brain throws a full-blown "what if" parade. It is about giving yourself permission to breathe. Worrying is natural, but it doesn't have to run the show. The mind loves to play the "what if" game. What if I fail? What if I mess up? What if I accidentally reply-all to the entire company? These thoughts can spiral faster than a toddler on sugar. One way to interrupt that spiral is to gently shift your focus to "What can I do right now?" That question brings you back to the present, where action lives. Maybe you can take one small step, send one email, drink some water, or just lie down and stare at the ceiling like a philosopher in sweatpants. Even the tiniest action can break the loop of helplessness.

Stopping mental anguish isn't about silencing your thoughts with metaphorical duct tape; it is about softening them. You can acknowledge your fears without feeding them a three-course meal. You can say, "I see you, worry," and then choose to do something grounding. Take a walk. Talk to a friend. Write things down. Sit quietly and breathe like you are auditioning for inner peace. These small acts remind your nervous system that you are safe and that you are not alone in whatever you are facing.

When you combine steady effort with a lighter mental load, you create a rhythm that is both productive and sustainable. You focus on what you can control—your attitude, your choices, your pace—and let go of the pressure to have it all figured out by Tuesday. This mindset doesn't just improve performance. It nurtures well-being. You sleep better, think more clearly, and enjoy life more. You become someone who moves with intention, not anxiety.

So yes, work hard. Push yourself to grow, to learn, to contribute. But also give yourself grace. Rest when you need to. Laugh when you can. Let go of the weight that doesn't belong to you. Life isn't a test you have to ace; it is a journey you get to shape. And the best way to shape it is with effort, compassion, and just enough ease to keep your spirit intact. And maybe a snack in your pocket, just in case.

XTRAS

The Xtras are quotes I've picked up along the way—some wise, some witty, all worth a peek. I hope one of them hits the spot, like finding a sticky note on your fridge with exactly the reminder you needed. You might try reading one a day or picking one at random, kind of like a fortune cookie, but with fewer calories and more insight.

- Open your heart and love more.
- Laugh more. Laughter is the best medicine.
- Boundaries aren't walls; they are doors with locks you control.
- If it costs you peace, it's too expensive.
- Not every battle is yours to fight.
- Healing means choosing peace over patterns.
- Say no without guilt and yes without apology.
- Let go of what weighs down your spirit.
- Sometimes the best way to offer support is to allow others to vent without jumping in.
- Your story isn't over just because a chapter was painful.
- The past is a place of reference, not residence.

- Scars remind us of where we've been, not who we are.
- In an argument, ask yourself, "Do I want to be right, or do I want to be happy?"
- Feed your mind good stuff. If your thoughts were food, would you eat them?
- Your body isn't a battleground; it is your lifelong dance partner. Treat it like someone you love.
- You don't need a detox; you need a daily dose of self-compassion.
- Treat your mind like an empty canvas each morning because the moment you think it's full, you stop painting.
- Don't burn bridges. You never know when you'll need to travel on it again.
- Seeking therapy isn't a sign of being broken; it's a sign of being brave enough to grow.
- Stay curious about your blind spots, grateful for your growth, and open to being wrong because humility isn't shrinking; it's expanding beyond ego.
- Your body's not being dramatic; it's dropping hints. Tune in before it starts sending voice memos.
- Judgment builds walls. Compassion builds bridges.
- Never compare yourself to others. It's a waste of energy. You are unique and have your own gifts to offer the world.
- Don't stress so much over decisions. Decisions don't need to be forever.
- When overwhelmed, ask yourself, "Will this even be an issue in five years?"
- Everything we hear is an opinion, not a fact. Everything we see is a perspective, not the truth.
- Magic happens outside your comfort zone.
- Listen more; talk less.
- Laugh until your abs hurt. Boom. Free core workout.

- Unfollow anyone who treats you like a side salad. You're the main course with dessert energy, extra whipped, zero apologies.
- "Whatever comes, let it come, whatever stays, let it stay, whatever goes, let it go. Just flow and trust that I got your back." -The Universe.

While many of the following quotes are widely associated with Oprah Winfrey, it's important to note that not all may have originated directly from her. Over time, powerful words often get shared, paraphrased, and attributed to influential voices like Oprah. Whether she said each one verbatim or simply inspired the sentiment, the wisdom still resonates, reminding us to live with intention, courage, and grace.

- "Be thankful for what you have; you'll end up having more. If you concentrate on what you don't have, you will never, ever have enough."
- "Let excellence be your brand. When you are excellent, you become unforgettable."
- "Doing the best at this moment puts you in the best place for the next moment."
- "Turn your wounds into wisdom."
- "Real integrity is doing the right thing, knowing that nobody's going to know whether you did it or not."
- "The more you praise and celebrate your life, the more there is in life to celebrate."
- "Challenges are gifts that force us to search for a new center of gravity. Don't fight them. Just find a new way to stand."
- "I trust that everything happens for a reason, even when we're not wise enough to see it."

- "Only make decisions that support your self-image, self-esteem, and self-worth."
- "Surround yourself with only people who are going to lift you higher."
- "Passion is energy. Feel the power that comes from focusing on what excites you."
- "You get in life what you have the courage to ask for."
- "Breathe. Let go. And remind yourself that this very moment is the only one you know you have for sure."
- "With every experience, you alone are painting your own canvas, thought by thought, choice by choice."
- "The key to realizing a dream is to focus not on success but on significance."

Y

YOUR TRIBE

Finding true friends, your ride-or-die tribe, is one of the most essential (and occasionally hilarious) parts of the human experience. Whether it's a cozy duo who finish your sentences or a full-blown entourage that rivals a reality show cast (minus the drama, please), these are the people who truly get you. They cheer for your wins like they've got stock in your success, and they show up with tissues, tacos, or tequila when life throws curveballs.

True friends are those rare unicorns who let you be your gloriously weird, wonderfully authentic self with no masks, no filters, no need to pretend that you like kale. They're the ones who laugh with you until you snort, cry with you without judgment, and remind you that you're not alone in this wild ride called life.

The secret sauce to finding your tribe is that you've got to become the kind of person you want to attract. Want friends who are kind, curious, and emotionally intelligent? Start by being that. Want people who can handle your quirks and call you out with love? Be that mirror. The universe has a funny way of matching energy. So if you're radiating authenticity, compassion, and a dash of sass, your tribe will find you like dogs sniffing out treats

—instinctively, joyfully, and with tail-wagging enthusiasm. They will know where the good energy lives.

Get involved in things that light you up, whether it's a book club, a beach clean-up, or a dance class where nobody knows the steps, but everyone's vibing anyway. When you show up as your real self in spaces that reflect your values, you naturally attract kindred spirits who speak your language, whether that's fluent sarcasm, deep soul talk, or both.

Building these friendships takes effort, patience, and the occasional awkward text that says, "Hey, I really like you as a human." It means showing up, listening deeply, and being willing to navigate the messy bits with grace. Communication is your compass, empathy is your map, and humor is your fuel.

True friends are not just companions; they're your chosen family. They make the highs higher, the lows bearable, and the in-betweens full of meaning. So, become the vibe you want to attract, and trust that your tribe is out there, probably wondering where you've been all their lives.

Z

ZOOM INTO THERAPY

There was a time when therapy meant sitting in a waiting room, pretending to read a magazine from 2008 while silently hoping no one recognized you. Now you can Zoom into therapy from your couch, your car, or the one quiet corner of your home that doesn't echo like a cave. Therapy has never been more accessible or more powerful.

Zooming into therapy is not a sign that you are falling apart; it is a sign that you are tuning in. You are choosing to pause the chaos and say, let me check in with myself before I spiral into a dramatic monologue about why my coworker's punctuation ruined my day. That is not weakness; that is wisdom. You are not hiding from your problems. You are logging in to face them, one awkward silence and one deep sigh at a time. Therapy is sanity maintenance.

When you have a toothache, you visit a dentist. If your knee starts clicking like an untuned piano, you go to a doctor. So why not seek a bit more guidance when life feels like a tornado in a laundry basket? A good therapist who fits your needs can help you see things from a new angle, untangle the emotional knots, and make sense of the chaos. Therapy is not just about talking; it is about transforming.

Therapy is not for people who are crazy. People who are truly off the rails rarely think they need help. Therapy is for people who want to grow. It is for those who are brave enough to say they want to understand themselves better, they want to break cycles, or they want to stop reacting like a raccoon in a thunderstorm every time someone criticizes them. Therapy is not a weakness; it is a strategy. It is emotional strength training with a licensed spotter.

So, walk into a therapy session without feeling like you need to whisper about it. You are not broken; you are evolving. You are choosing to expand your horizons, unpack your emotional attic, and maybe even dust off a little compassion for yourself. Therapy helps you sort through the clutter: those old beliefs, those reactive behaviors, those stories you tell yourself that no longer serve you. It is not about fixing you; it is about freeing you. Those beliefs and behaviors were formed when you were a child, and they might have served you then, but they surely are not serving you now.

So, if you are in therapy, thinking about therapy, or just Googled why you cry when someone says, "We need to talk," congratulations. You are doing the work. You are choosing growth over stagnation, clarity over confusion, and healing over hiding. That is not crazy; that is courageous. What do you have to lose? Nothing but the weight that no longer serves you. And what do you have to gain? Clarity, growth, peace, and a life that finally makes sense. You deserve the very best because that is your birthright, and don't allow anyone to tell you otherwise.

FUNNY STORIES

Yes, this is a true story. The girl in the picture with one lens on and one lens off, wandering downtown Miami like a confused pirate on unpaid leave, that was me. I roamed the streets for over half an hour, blissfully unaware that I was serving strong "optical chaos meets urban chic" vibes.

Stress had me so frazzled, I didn't even notice. My coworkers nearly collapsed when I walked back into the office.

Lesson learned: when life gets blurry, check your lenses, and maybe your calendar, your coffee intake, and your cortisol levels while you're at it.

2

So back in my dating days, I moonlighted as a full-blown detective. Not the trench coat kind, more like the "let me run your name through every criminal, civil, and family court database before I let you buy me lunch" kind. I wasn't just dating; I was conducting background checks with the intensity of a CIA clearance.

One day, I get a hit. The guy who's supposed to take me to lunch? Married. I was so disappointed. He was so cute. So I'm gearing up for confrontation like a soldier prepping for battle, emotional grenades loaded, lots of extra rounds. I was so ready to shoot him down.

He walks into the office, all casual and charming, and I escort him to the kitchen for what I thought was a private showdown. But as I'm about to launch my verbal missiles, I glance under the door and see shoes, multiple shoes. My coworkers, bless their nosy hearts, had front-row seats to the drama.

For ten full minutes, I let him have it.

"How dare you?"

"What kind of man does this?"

"Do I look like a fool to you?"

The whole monologue. He just stands there and then starts laughing. Not nervous chuckles, but full comedy club laughter. Like I'd just performed a stand-up set titled "Dating Disasters."

He pulls out his license, his ID, even some credit cards for good measure to show me that I ran the wrong person.

It turns out, I had the wrong date of birth. It wasn't him. I had interrogated the wrong man and was ready to take him down.

And then more giggles.

Those sneaky shoes outside the door? Cracking up.

My coworkers had been eavesdropping like it was the season finale of *The Real Housewives of Miami.*

3

One of my coworkers, whose identity shall remain protected for their own social survival, had a talent for unintentionally starring in workplace bloopers. But the crown jewel of her "oops" collection?

Asking a woman how far along she was when she wasn't pregnant.

4

Another funny moment was in a medical doctor deposition. Imagine the scene: a solemn deposition, the air thick with legal tension, and then, out of nowhere, she drops the broccoli bomb. "So, Doctor, would you say ovaries are like broccoli? Do they grow in later?" I still have no idea what she meant by that. Actually, I don't think she still has any idea what she meant by that.

5

It was a regular afternoon at the office. The sun was shining, the printers were jamming, and one of the reporters had just politely declined a request for spare change from a local gentleman of unpredictable temperament. She thought that was the end of it. She thought wrong. Later, she heads out to her car, keys in hand, ready to drive off into the sunset, or at least into rush hour. But what's that? A mysterious mound on the hood. A gift. A statement. A steaming symbol of rejection. Yes. A turd. Not metaphorical. Not symbolic. A literal turd. The man had taken "leave behind" to a whole new level. Forget flowers. Forget notes. This was his version of a gift. And the poor reporter? She stood there, frozen between horror and hysterics, trying to decide whether to call animal control, a priest, or just torch the car and start over.

6

It's a medical trial. The doctor is on the stand, calmly explaining anatomy with the precision of someone who's memorized every Latin root in existence. Suddenly, mid-testimony, he pauses and says, "Oh, by the way, tell your colleague she spelled *penis* wrong in the transcript." And that colleague? Me. Guilty as charged.

Back then, no autocorrect. No red squiggly lines. Just raw phonetics and a dash of guesswork. And in that moment, *penus* was born. A spelling that sounds like it belongs in a botanical garden catalog. I wanted to vanish into my steno machine and emerge in a different profession. But instead, I took it like a champ, because only someone with my humor and humility could turn a typo into a timeless tale.

7

Everyone's scarfing down food like the jury's about to come back with a verdict. One court reporter starts clearing her throat like she's auditioning for a one-woman opera. She insists something is stuck in her throat. We, with a lot of sarcasm, offer water, a banana, and unsolicited advice. "You're fine. If you can talk, you can breathe. If you can breathe, you can work." Four hours later, she's still sounding like a human kazoo, and now she's Googling "why does my throat feel like a salad bar?" Turns out that an onion slice had lodged itself like a stubborn witness refusing to testify. After four hours of throat drama and unsolicited banana therapy, our brave court reporter finally gets medical help. The onion, clearly auditioning for a role in a musical, refuses to budge. Doctors sedate her to push it down. The plot twist: she's unknowingly allergic to anesthesia. She wakes up in a fog, greeted by her husband's face, a mix of concern, confusion, and a "what did you do now?" Turns out, in her loopy post-anesthesia state, she'd gone full Oprah in the ER: "You're invited! And you're invited! Everyone's invited to my fortieth birthday bash!" She even promised cake, karaoke, and a bounce house. Thank goodness only one nurse showed up after the court reporter issued numerous invitations. Still has no memory of it all.

8

One court reporter generously lent her steno machine case to her teenage daughter for a weekend trip. No big deal, right? Fast forward to Monday morning: she's back in court, the room is packed, and all eyes are on her as she walks in. She pops open the case to set up her machine, and out tumbles her daughter's thong. Yep. Right there in front of the judge, attorneys, and a jury that suddenly forgot what they were deliberating. Let's just say the transcript didn't capture the gasp, but the moment was unforgettable.

9

It was one of those days at the office, everyone buried in transcripts, caffeine running low, and stress running high. The mailman popped in with his usual cheerful hello, and we barely looked up. A few minutes later, someone asked, "Did we get any checks in the mail?" And there went the scavenger hunt. We tore through desks, checked under piles of paperwork, even peeked behind the copier like it owed us money. Ten minutes of collective confusion later, we gave up and went back to work. Then one of the reporters opened the fridge for a drink, and there it was. The mail. Sitting next to someone's salad like it belonged there. Turns out, in the frenzy, one of us gave the mail a time-out in the fridge, because apparently, even envelopes need to chill sometimes.

10

The father of one of my best friends passed away. She's of Haitian descent, and when she told me the name of the funeral parlor, I, being the confident little GPS rebel that I am, assumed it was the one in my city. (Yes, I know. Assumptions: the gateway drug to public humiliation.)

So, my partner and I head over, dressed respectfully, emotionally prepared, and slightly hungry. I had promised him we'd grab dinner right after. He was already dreaming of empanadas and a glass of wine. We walk into the funeral home, and I immediately notice I'm the only Latina girl in the room. Everyone is singing and praying. It's a beautiful celebration of life. My partner whispers, "Wait, babe," but I ignore him because clearly I'm on a mission. I start walking toward the casket, assuming (again!) that my girlfriend is up front mourning her dad.

People are looking at me like I just wandered in from a different movie. I get to the casket, and it's a woman. Not my friend's dad. Not even close. I look back at my partner, and his eyes are halfway out of his skull, silently screaming, "Abort mission!"

I call my girlfriend in a panic, and she says, "Girl, you're in the wrong city."

Wrong City. Not the wrong room. Not the wrong building. The wrong ZIP code.

So, we hop back in the car and drive forty-five minutes to the correct funeral home. I laughed the entire ride over, like, full belly laugh with the occasional cackle. My partner, however, was not amused. He was angry, hungry, and emotionally exhausted from watching me crash a stranger's funeral like a confused telenovela character. And now, thanks to my detour, I'd added another hour to the mix. The empanadas were a distant dream.

Moral of the story? Never assume.

And never promise food to a hungry man unless you've triple-checked the GPS and packed snacks for emotional emergencies.

11

During a deposition, the conversation took an unexpected turn toward the individual's sense of smell. Somewhere in the transcript, the court reporter recorded the term "old factory," which, while it does sound like a place where antique furniture goes to retire, was clearly a mishearing of olfactory, the correct term for anything related to the sense of smell. The olfactory system helps us detect odors, from fresh-baked cookies to questionable leftovers. This charming typo serves as a gentle reminder that even in serious settings, a single syllable can send us sniffing in entirely the wrong direction. The attorney thought that "old factory" deserved prime real estate, so he hung it on his door and turned the hallway into a comedy show. Of course, he erased the court reporter's name. I will give him that.

12

Despite being a young mother of two, a very naïve court reporter found herself in a moment of pure transcript confusion during a police detective's deposition. After hearing the word "dildo," she leaned in and asked, quite sincerely, "What's that?" The attorney and detective exchanged a glance, clearly puzzled, but then noticed her genuinely perplexed expression and kindly began to explain. As the explanation unfolded, the poor reporter started turning redder than a stop sign at rush hour. It was like watching a prairie dog slowly realize it's being watched, head halfway down, unsure whether to commit to full burrow or brave the moment.

A clear and classic case of "I wish I hadn't asked."

13

Taking a detective's deposition again, I showed up bundled in a scarf because it was freezing outside. Well, it was Florida's version of "cold," which means anything under 65 degrees. But halfway through, my neck turned into a furnace. I didn't want to interrupt, so I started unraveling my scarf quietly like a magician pulling silk from a sleeve—a little at a time so no one would notice.

The detective looked at me, raised an eyebrow, stopped the deposition, and asked, "Are you having a moment?"

Excuse me? A moment? Was he calling me old? I was in my mid-forties, thank you very much. How dare he?

Turns out I really was having a moment. Early menopause had entered the chat.

And just when I thought the deposition couldn't get any more awkward, the finale arrived: at the end, the detective asked me out on a date.

I said no out of pure, hormonal spite.

14

I was twenty years old, fresh out of court reporting school, so shy I practically apologized to doorways for walking through them. I started interning at a firm that was desperate for reporters—like, "throw her in the deep end and hope she floats" desperate.

They sent me out to cover what was supposed to be a short hearing. I show up, and surprise! It's a full-blown jury trial. The only thing I knew about jury trials was what I'd seen on *Law & Order*, and even then, I was mostly focused on the dramatic music.

At one point, the judge said, "We're having a sidebar." Both attorneys walk up to the bench like they're in on some secret club. I stay seated, clutching my machine like it's a flotation device.

The judge looks over and says, "Ma'am, we're having a sidebar." I nod politely and say, "Okay, Judge," like I'm giving him permission.

Third time's the charm: he looks me dead in the eye and says, "We need you up here."

Cue me scrambling like a squirrel in traffic, dragging cords and confusion behind me. I was so clueless, I might as well have been wearing a sign that said, "First day on Earth."

Embarrassing? Yes. Character-building? Also, yes. And now? Laughing material for this book.

15

I started court reporting back in the Stone Age. (Just kidding, I'm not that old). But let's just say our machines weren't digital. They recorded everything on paper, and that paper was sacred. Lose it, and you might as well lose your job, your sanity, and your will to live.

Once, after a marathon day of stenography and caffeine, my coworker and I were walking to our cars in downtown Miami. Suddenly, her briefcase popped open like a jack-in-the-box, and out came her entire pack of notes flying down the street like confetti at a legal parade.

We had to stop traffic and chase those notes. We performed a full-blown paper rescue operation. She was so nervous, she looked like she was defusing a bomb as she rolled each sheet back up.

It was like watching a slow-motion scene from a courtroom-themed action movie: "The Notes or Your Life." Papers flying, traffic halting, adrenaline pumping.

And yes, we lived to report another day or, in my case, another thirty-five years of stenographic survival.

16

I'm in a jury trial, dressed to impress in a very nice skirt suit—professional, poised, and ready to report. I'm seated in one of those armchairs that looks innocent enough … until it turns into a wardrobe assassin.

My skirt had a modest slit in the back, but when I stood up, that slit said "I quit" and caught on the chair arm, ripping all the way up to my waist.

Houston, we had a problem.

My behind was suddenly making a surprise appearance, and let's just say it's not the kind you can discreetly tuck away. We still had hours to go, and shockingly, no one in the courthouse had a needle and thread. So, what did I do? I marched into a private room, took off my skirt, and stapled the seams back together like I was assembling a legal document.

And then I sat on staples for hours. Every shift in my seat felt like a paper cut to the soul. But I finished that trial with dignity, discomfort, and a newfound respect for office supplies.

17

I was officiating a small, dreamy wedding ceremony—picture-perfect lake behind me, twinkling lights, flowers everywhere. It was the kind of setting that makes you whisper "wow" even when you're the one talking.

I'm standing there, performing the ceremony with grace and poise, and at the end, it's time to notarize the paperwork.

Now, this was one of those old-school notary seals, the kind you have to squeeze like you're juicing a lemon to leave an imprint. I press down, and instead of the satisfying click, I hear a crunch. Not the snacky kind, but the bug kind.

Turns out, a bug had crawled inside the seal, and I unknowingly gave it the stamp of doom.

The couple's official marriage license now featured a decorative bug splatter right across the seal. Romantic? Not exactly.

I got so nervous, I spiraled into a full-blown laugh attack. The kind where you try to hide behind your hair, but your shoulders are shaking and your eyes are watering.

The bride and groom saw everything. Everyone else just thought I was overcome with emotion, or mildly unhinged.

Moral of the story: If it's important, edible-looking, or vaguely hollow, don't leave it unattended near a lake. Bugs are opportunists with zero boundaries and impeccable timing.

18

Three of us were headed to a retreat in Kansas.

One of us, who shall remain nameless but knows who they are, was in charge of booking the flights and transportation.

Everything seemed fine until we got a message that the house we were headed to was …wait for it … three and a half hours from the airport.

Not because it was tucked away in some mystical forest or hidden behind a secret corn maze. Nope. Just a classic case of "Oops, wrong airport," and by the time we realized it, the plane was basically boarding.

So, we did what any group of mildly panicked, slightly sleep-deprived travelers would do: we rented a car and embarked on a three-hour tour through the majestic cornfields of Kansas.

It was like a road trip sponsored by popcorn.

We laughed, we bonded, and we definitely saw more corn than any human should in one sitting.

We had a choice to get mad, and we could have, but instead we chose adventure.

Because sometimes the best memories come from the wrong airport and a whole lot of corn.

19

So there I was at Costco, three months postpartum, pushing a stroller with my actual baby inside, like, visible proof that the pregnancy had ended. I run into an old friend who skips the small talk and goes straight for, "When are you due?"

I blinked. I looked at her. I looked at the stroller. I looked back at her. And said, "The baby is in the stroller."

Her face did a full color wheel, red, white, green, and she even looked like she stopped breathing. It was a moment of "let earth swallow me and let me disappear forever." I wasn't offended. I mean, sure, I still had a belly and plenty of weight, but I also had a whole human to show for it. I just laughed and let her stew in her own awkward soup.

And hey, three months later, I lost all the baby weight. So really, the only thing I carried from that moment was the memory, and maybe a jumbo pack of diapers.

Now, my girlfriend? She took it to the next level. She asked a client when she was due, but the client wasn't pregnant and hadn't recently given birth. She was just living her life. That's not just putting your foot in your mouth; that's setting up a tent and camping there (which she often did).

Some moments are cringey. Others are legendary. This one? A little bit of both.

20

Picture this: a sunny afternoon, two hungry ladies, and a hunter green van with dreams of flame-grilled glory. My girlfriend and I are in the Burger King drive-thru, chatting like caffeinated parrots on a podcast. We're deep in conversation, probably some juicy gossip, when *BANG!* followed by the unmistakable sound of metal giving up on life.

Ladies and gentlemen, I had just introduced my van to the bright yellow pole designed to keep reckless drivers like me from turning the restaurant into a drive-in. Mission accomplished, pole. You win this round.

The back of my van now looked like it had been kissed by a radioactive banana.

I tried to reverse, but the car responded with a symphony of crunches that sounded like Optimus Prime chewing aluminum foil. So, I did what any panicked person would do: I floored it forward like I was escaping a zombie apocalypse.

Once we cleared the pole, I got out to assess the damage. The van now had a dent so deep it could hold guacamole. My girlfriend, ever the optimist, hops out with a single Kleenex like she's about to erase a crime scene.

I told her, "Unless that tissue is dipped in magic, get back in the car." Except my words were a bit more colorful and not so nice. We laughed so hard we probably scared the guy handing out Whoppers.

I wasn't giggling so much when I handed over $1,500 to fix what was essentially a fast-food fender bender. Moral of the story? If you're going to crash into something, make sure it's not color-coded for maximum humiliation. And maybe next time, we'll walk to Burger King.

21

We were fifteen strong, marching into the Florida Keys like a traveling circus for Lobster Fest. Six couples, two single girls (me included), and one last-minute gentleman who immediately started orbiting my friend like she was the moon.

The couples all had their private rooms. The three singles? We got the "playroom" on the third floor—translation: one lumpy sofa and a kingsize bed. We looked at each other, shrugged, and said, "Eh, we're small people. Three in a bed? No big deal."

So there we were, tucked under the covers, cracking jokes like it was a slumber party. Then—silence. A pause. And suddenly... *Pffffft.*

My sweet, classy, quiet friend had betrayed us. At first, nobody reacted. Maybe nobody heard it. Maybe we were all being polite. But then the gentleman, trying to be gallant, lifted the sheet to cover himself.

Big mistake.

He gagged. Loudly. Like a man choking on a lobster claw. I caught a whiff and immediately joined him, gagging between bursts of laughter.

Me: "Oh my God—what is that?!"

Him: "It's … it's … weaponized!"

My friend: frozen, eyes wide, not moving a muscle. She looked like she was bracing for impact in a submarine.

The smell was so bad we had to evacuate. Picture three adults, sprinting out of a bedroom at midnight, collapsing on the stairs, laughing so hard we couldn't breathe.

It took us an hour to stop laughing, another hour to work up the courage to reenter the room.

The story became legendary. One of the guys was a radio newscaster, and he told it on air—no names, but enough detail that everyone in our group knew exactly who the "culprit" was.

And the gentleman who had been courting her? He was a saint. He told her, "Don't worry. It happens to everyone." Which is true. But not everyone leaves a lasting impression that clears a room faster than a fire alarm.

To this day, we still laugh about it. Lobster Fest may have been the destination, but the real show was the night of the silent but deadly.

22

I was strutting down the courthouse stairs, briefcase in one hand, purse in the other, feeling like a boss. That is, until my heel got lodged in a broken tile like it owed rent. I squirmed, twisted, and performed what can only be described as a solo interpretive dance to free it.

And then—*bam!* My heel launched like a heat-seeking missile and struck an innocent bystander squarely in the chest. The poor man looked stunned, I looked mortified, and for a moment we both froze in a silent courtroom drama.

Then came the laughter. His face said, "Did that just happen?" Mine said, "Please let the ground swallow me." But instead, we both cracked up as I limped down the stairs to retrieve my rogue shoe, dignity trailing behind me.

America's Funniest Videos? Missed opportunity. But hey, I nailed the landing.

ABOUT THE AUTHOR

Dania Alen is a psychology-trained executive and personal coach with a Bachelor of Science in Psychology (Child Development) and a Master's in Clinical Applications of Transpersonal Psychology. Based in Coral Gables, Florida, she works with individuals, couples, and both personal and business groups who want to communicate more effectively, reduce reactivity, and lead with confidence and intention.

Her work centers on teaching people how to regulate their nervous system so they can stay grounded under pressure, avoid the drama triangle, and show up as their best selves in every setting. Whether she's supporting a couple strengthening their connection or a leadership team navigating organizational stress, Dania helps clients release unproductive patterns and build healthier, more effective ways of relating—with compassion at the core of every step.

In group and organizational environments, she focuses on team dynamics, stress responses, and the subtle patterns that quietly undermine performance. Her programs strengthen collaboration, improve engagement, and support cultures where people feel steady, respected, and aligned.

Dania guides individuals and teams through meaningful transformation, helping them understand and regulate their internal operating system so they can unlock a level of performance—and possibility—that elevates every part of their life and work. Her approach blends clarity with heart, reminding people that growth is not just strategic, but deeply human.

www.ingramcontent.com/pod-product-compliance
Lightning Source LLC
Chambersburg PA
CBHW071215130726
47998CB00002B/759